Headway

Academic Skills

Listening, Speaking, and Study Skills

LEVEL 2 **Student's Book**

University of Brighton | International College

Sarah Philpot and Lesley Curnick
Series Editors: Liz and John Soars

OXFORD

CONTENTS

1 Moving on

LISTENING SKILLS How to listen • Factors which affect listening
SPEAKING SKILLS Formal, neutral, and informal language • Asking for repetition
VOCABULARY DEVELOPMENT Word stress (1) • Using a dictionary (1) and (2)

LISTENING New places, new people

1 Who and what do you listen to? Complete the table. Work with a partner and compare your ideas.

for education	for general information	for pleasure
	radio news	

2 **Read STUDY SKILL**

> **STUDY SKILL** How to listen
>
> When you study, the way you listen depends on *why* you are listening. Decide if you are:
> - listening for the general idea, e.g. the speaker's opinion, the main point(s) of a talk
> - listening selectively for detail(s), e.g. a name, a date, a time
> - listening intensively for a lot of information, e.g. to take notes from a lecture

Read the notice below. You have arrived at a new university. There is a talk for all new overseas students. You want to know:

1 What is the purpose of the talk?
2 What are the three main topics?
What sort of information do you need? How are you going to listen?

> ### OVERSEAS STUDENTS' GROUP
>
> The welcome meeting with the Senior Tutor will be held in
> Lecture Theatre B3 at 10 a.m. on Wednesday 10th.

3 🔘 1.1 Listen and answer questions 1 and 2 in exercise 2.

4 Look at questions 1–4 below. What sort of information do you need? How are you going to listen?
1 What is the name of the speaker?
2 Where is Mrs Roberts's office?
3 Why would you go to Dr Reynolds?
4 Name two things that you need to register at the medical centre.

5 🔘 1.1 Listen again and answer the questions in exercise 4.

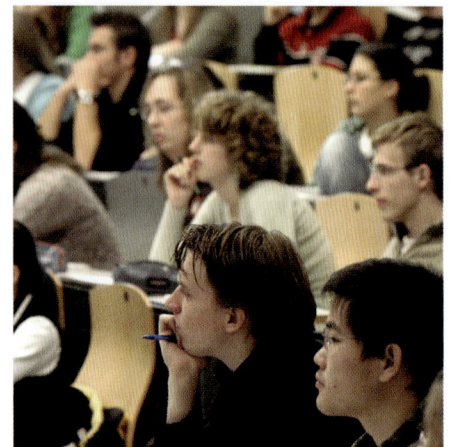

6 Complete the notes from the talk.

Introductions:	Dr Green – Senior Tutor – ¹_____ students
	next couple of weeks – ²_____ individually
Practical things:	accommodation – Mrs ³_____ / Room 214 Senate Building
	money – Dr Reynolds, St. Financial Adviser / Room 117 Admin Block
	NB make an ⁴_____
	health – medical centre next to Admin.
	⁵_____ as soon as possible!
	Receptionist – details, passport, student card

7 ⏺ 1.1 Listen again and check your answers.

What makes listening difficult?

8 ⏺ 1.2 Listen and put extracts a–e in the order you hear them.

a ☐ an announcement ____
b ☐ a conversation ____
c ☐ a survey ____
d ☐ a lecture ____
e ☐ a radio news item ____

9 ⏺ 1.2 Listen again and put the extracts from exercise 8 in order from 1 (the easiest to understand) to 5 (the most difficult to understand). Compare your answers with a partner.

10 **Read STUDY SKILL** What made the listening extracts difficult? Add your ideas to the diagram.

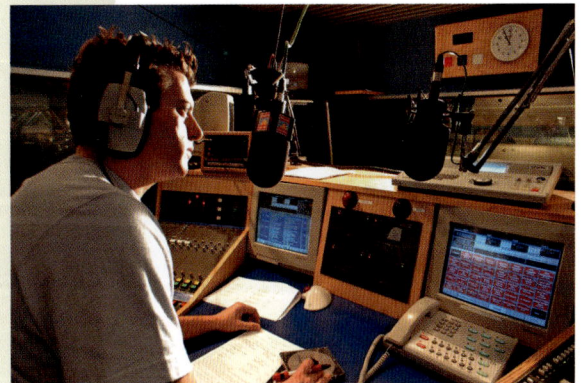

A radio news announcer

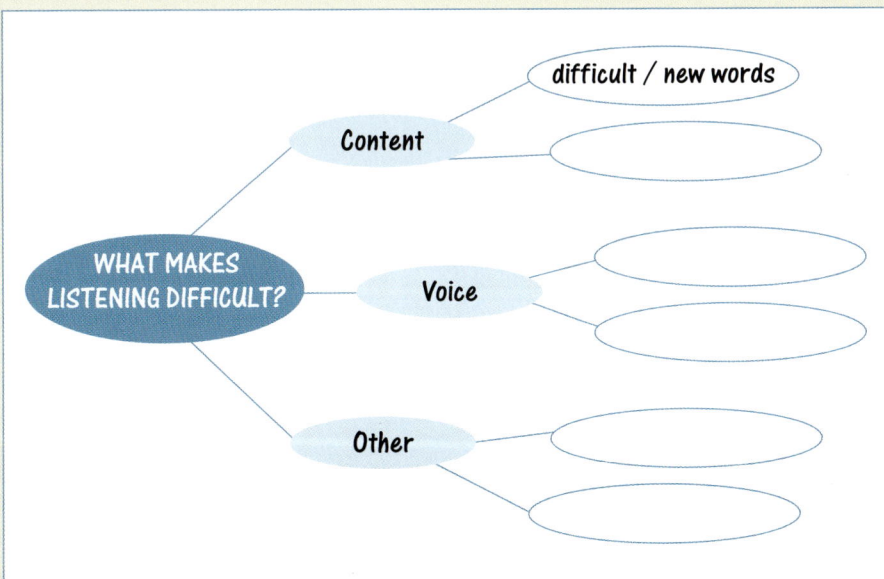

STUDY SKILL
Factors which affect listening

There are things which can make listening difficult. Predict what these will be and think about how to help yourself.

For example, usually in a lecture you only hear the information once, and cannot interrupt or ask for clarification.

Think about the topic of the lecture and predict the content.

Study any visual aids for extra information.

```
                              ( difficult / new words )
                    ( Content )
                              (            )
( WHAT MAKES
LISTENING DIFFICULT? )
                              (            )
                    ( Voice )
                              (            )

                              (            )
                    ( Other )
                              (            )
```

Discuss your ideas in groups.

SPEAKING Introductions

1 `Read STUDY SKILL` 🎧 1.3 Listen to some people introducing themselves. Decide if they are being formal (F), neutral (N), or informal (I).

1 ___   2 ___   3 ___   4 ___   5 ___

> ### STUDY SKILL Formal, neutral, and informal language
>
> When you introduce yourself to a colleague or classmate, be informal.
> Use: *Hello / Hi / Morning* and give your first name.
> *Hello, I'm Fatima.*
>
> When you introduce yourself to someone more senior, be more formal.
> Use your title or their title, and your family name.
> *Good morning, may I introduce myself? I am Professor Armstrong.*
>
> If you do not know if you should be formal or informal, be neutral.
> Use: *Hello / Good morning / afternoon* and give your first and family name.
> *Hello, my name's Alan Masters.*

2 Work with a partner. Introduce yourselves to each other.

Student **A**
Your partner is:
1 your new professor
2 someone attending a conference you are at

Student **B**
Your partner is:
3 a new classmate
4 a guest lecturer

3 🎧 1.4 Listen to people introducing themselves in a tutorial. Complete the table.

name of student	city and country	studies / interests / plans
1 Dilek Sancak	Turkey	Accountancy and Finance
2 Sachit Malhotra		
3 Mahmoud Subri		

4 Work in groups. Introduce yourself. Greet your classmates and say:
- who you are
- where you come from
- what you are studying and why

Exchanging information

5 Look at the symbols used in email and web addresses. Label the web address with the words we use for the symbols.

| underscore   forward slash   hyphen   dot   at |

greg_man-wright@mailnet.com/finance

1 _____   2 _____   3 _____   4 _____   5 _____

6 🎧 1.5 Listen and complete the email and web addresses.

1 emily.shaw_____

2 _____.grant_____liv.ac._____

3 _____.reddy_____public_____

4 buzz _____nsw_____

5 _____mech-eng

7 Read STUDY SKILL 🎧 1.6 Read and listen to the conversations. Underline the phrases that ask for information to be repeated or clarified.

1 **A** Give me a ring on my mobile. The number's 076532215.
  B Did you say two two one five?
  A Yeah, two two one five.

2 **A** Let me make a note of your email address.
  B Sure. It's alan.rodgers13@uwe.ac.uk.
  A Was that thirteen or thirty?
  B Thirteen, one three.

3 **A** Good morning, this is Ella Peters speaking. Is that Chang Li?
  B Yes, it is. Sorry, this is a bad line. I didn't catch your name.
  A Ella, Ella Peters. We met at the conference last week.

4 **A** It's Paul. Can I pop round and return that book I borrowed? Where's your room?
  B It's Bowland Tower, room nine on the third floor.
  A Third floor?
  B Yeah.

5 **A** The best person on this subject is Dr Shehadeh and I advise you to read her latest article.
  B Sorry, could you repeat the name, please?
  A Certainly, Dr Shehadeh, that's S…h…e…h…a…d…e…h.

8 Complete the table with information about you.

name	mobile or landline number	email address
Your name		
Partner 1		
Partner 2		
Partner 3		
Partner 4		

9 Work with different partners. Exchange information about yourselves and complete the table in exercise 8. Ask for repetition, using expressions in the Language Bank.

LANGUAGE BANK
Expressions for asking for repetition

Informal	Formal
I didn't catch …	*Could you repeat …?*
Pardon?	*Could you say … again?*
What was that?	*Sorry / Excuse me, did you say …?*
Did you say …?	*Sorry / Excuse me, was that …?*
Was that …?	

VOCABULARY DEVELOPMENT   Word stress

1 Read STUDY SKILL   1.7 Listen to the words. Underline the stressed syllables. Say the words aloud.

1 <u>de</u>tail
2 advise
3 campus
4 mobile
5 thirteen
6 thirty
7 return
8 passport
9 account
10 repeat

STUDY SKILL   Word stress (1)

In words with two or more syllables, one syllable will be stressed, e.g. <u>rea</u>son. Other syllables are less pronounced. Often the unstressed vowel sounds are changed to a schwa /ə/, e.g. tea<u>cher</u> /tɪːtʃə(r)/. Saying words with the correct stress makes it easier for the listener to understand you.

2 1.8 Listen to the words. Underline the stressed syllable. Circle the schwa /ə/ sounds. Say the words aloud.

1 depend
2 tutor
3 accent
4 accept
5 lecture

Using a dictionary

3 Read STUDY SKILL   Underline the stressed syllable. Use a dictionary to help. Say the words aloud.

Verbs	Nouns
1 study	1 register
2 research	2 tutorial
3 present	3 visitor
4 debate	4 seminar
5 discuss	5 finance

Silent letters

4 Look at the words below. What is the difference between the spelling and the pronunciation? Read STUDY SKILL

know _____   write _____   listen _____

5 Cross out the letters that are silent in the words in the box. Use a dictionary to help.

1 sign	4 island	7 business
2 right	5 guest	8 column
3 what	6 science	9 answer

1.9 Listen and check your answers.

campus
lecture
study
seminar
tutorial
tutor

STUDY SKILL   Using a dictionary (1)

A dictionary gives you information on pronouncing a word, e.g. *communicate* /kə'mjuːnɪkeɪt/.

communicate 🔑 AW /kə'mjuːnɪkeɪt/ *verb*
1 [I,T] to share and exchange information, ideas or feelings with sb: *Parents often have difficulty communicating with their teenage children.* ◇ *Our boss is good at communicating her ideas to the team.* **2** [T] (*formal*) (usually passive) HEALTH to pass a disease from one person or animal to another **3** [I] to lead from one place to another: *two rooms with a communicating door*

Always mark the stress on new vocabulary, e.g. *commu<u>ni</u>cate*

STUDY SKILL   Using a dictionary (2)

Some words in English have silent letters, that is, letters that are not pronounced, e.g. in *know* /nəʊ/, the letter '*k*' is silent.

know[1] 🔑 /nəʊ/ *verb* (*pt* **knew** /njuː/; *pp* **known** /nəʊn/) (not used in the continuous tenses) **1** [I,T] ~ (about sth); ~ that... to have knowledge or information in your mind: *I don't know much about sport.* ◇ *Do you know where this bus stops?* ◇ *Do you know their telephone number?* ◇ 'You've got a flat tyre.' 'I know.' ◇ *Do you* **know the way** *to the restaurant?* ◇ *Knowing Katie, she'll be out with her friends.* **2** [T] to

REVIEW

1 🔊 1.10 Listen to the introductions to two lectures. What subject are the lectures about?

Lecture 1 _____   Lecture 2 _____

2 🔊 1.11 Listen to Lecture 2 again and complete the notes.

LECTURER: Dr Knight	TUTORS
What does 'Bus. Management' mean?	Dr Knight – Head of _____ + Human Resources _____
1 _____ resources?	_____ – Finance and _____
2 _____ ?	Dr Williams – _____
3 _____ systems?	
NB and _____ aspects!	

3 Match each listening situation with two possible problems and one way of dealing with it.

situation	problems	strategies
1 Listening to an airport announcement 2 Listening to a conversation between three English friends 3 Listening to a lecture	a change of topic b hear once only c new / unknown vocabulary d quality of broadcasting system e speed of speech f understanding letters and numbers in English	i Listen for change of topic signposts, e.g. *By the way* and *Oh, that reminds me.* ii Listen for signposts such as *Firstly, Secondly.* iii Practise saying the flight number aloud.

4 Work with a partner or in small groups. Brainstorm other things you can do to make listening easier in each situation listed in exercise 3.

5 Complete the sentences using phrases from the box.

could you repeat   Did you say   Good morning   Hello   Hi   I didn't catch

1 _____ , Professor.
2 _____ , Susie!
3 _____ , I'm Ms Jones.
4 I'm sorry, Dr Adwan, _____ the name, please?
5 _____ John's room is on the second floor?
6 Sorry, Ella, _____ the name.

6 Mark the main stress on the words from the unit. Use a dictionary to help.

Nouns	**Verbs**	**Adjectives**
1 dictionary	4 arrive	7 formal
2 vocabulary	5 complete	8 informal
3 university	6 answer	9 neutral

7 Complete the questions below with a word from exercise 6. Work with a partner and take turns to ask and answer the questions.

1 Do you use an English–English _____ ?
2 Which _____ or college do you study at?
3 Where do you record new _____ ?
4 Do you understand the difference between _____ , _____ , and _____ language?

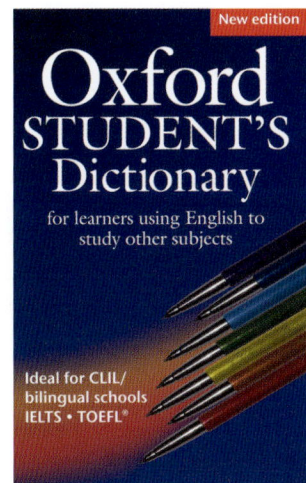

2 Island states

LISTENING Separated by water

1 Work with a partner. Look at the maps. Discuss what you know about the two countries. **Read STUDY SKILL**

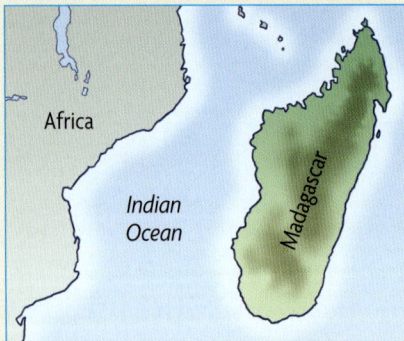
Map 1

Map 2

> **STUDY SKILL** Predicting content
>
> Predicting the content of a lecture or talk prepares you for listening. Being well prepared helps you understand. Before a talk:
> - think about the title or subject of the talk
> - think about what you already know about the subject
> - read about the subject before the lecture
> - think about what the important words and vocabulary will be

2 Read the handout for a lecture.

1 What will the lecturer discuss?

> ### Physical Geography and Economic Development (3): Island states
>
> The third lecture in this series will look at how being an island affects a country's economic development. We will look particularly at developments in agriculture and industry.
>
> Before the lecture, please read the following:
>
> Tiempo, G. (2009), *Economic Development in the Philippines*, Manila University Press, 5–11
> Rabinur, M. *The development of agricultural exports in Madagascar from 1879–2005*, 2010, December 4, http://countryprofiles.org/economy/index.html

2 Complete the table using the words in the box.

rice	coconuts
coffee	electronics
~~vanilla~~	~~food processing~~
maize	petroleum refining
mining	sugar cane

agricultural products	industries
vanilla,	food processing,

3 **Read STUDY SKILL** 🔊 2.1 Listen to the lecture and complete the tasks.

1 Number the countries in the order you hear them.

☐ the Philippines   ☐ Madagascar

2 Tick the main topics of the lecture.

☐ agriculture   ☐ location   ☐ physical geography
☐ climate   ☐ industry   ☐ population

> **STUDY SKILL** Listening for gist (1)
>
> It is important to understand the general ideas of a talk or lecture. This helps you understand how the detailed information is related.
> - listen for the topics, e.g. *Madagascar*
> - listen for the headings for each topic, e.g. *Location, Climate*

4 Read STUDY SKILL ⊚ 2.1 Listen again and complete the notes.

Physical Geography and Economic Development (3): Island states

   MADAGASCAR

Location – [1]_____ Ocean, east coast of Africa

Climate – coast – [2]_____ / south – dry

Physical geography – mountainous

Agriculture – main crops – [3]_____ / vanilla / [4]_____ / sugar cane

Industries – food processing / [5]_____ _____

   THE PHILIPPINES

Location – Pacific Ocean, S.E. [6]_____

Climate – tropical (wet / dry)

Physical geography – 7000+ [7]_____ / Luzon – mountains

Agriculture – crops – rice / maize / coconuts / [8]_____ _____

Industries – [9]_____ / petroleum refining / [10]_____ / food & drink processing.

STUDY SKILL Taking notes (1)

Taking good notes in a talk or lecture helps you record and remember important information. To make clear notes, use:

- headings e.g. *Location*, *Climate*, etc.
- numbers
- tables
- diagrams

5 Read STUDY SKILL ⊚ 2.2 Listen and complete the sentences.

1 _____ it is very mountainous, it's also very rich agriculturally.

2 It has a tropical climate _____ is dry in the south.

3 _____ , increased agriculture, mining, and the wood industry have led to deforestation.

6 ⊚ 2.3 Listen to the start of the sentences. Tick the correct ending.

1 a it has one of the longest coastlines in the world. ✓
   b it has a small population.

2 a it has one of the longest coastlines in the world.
   b it has a small population.

3 a more and more people are moving into industry.
   b produces 80% of the country's exports.

4 a more and more people are moving into industry.
   b produce 80% of the country's exports.

7 See the Language Bank. Complete the sentences with your own ideas.

1 Although English is an international language, _____ .

2 English is an international language and _____ .

3 The Internet is an important source of information. However,

   _____ .

4 The Internet is an important source of information, and

   _____ .

STUDY SKILL
Recognizing signposts (1)

Certain words tell you the type of information that will follow. Listening for these words will help you understand the direction of the talk or lecture, e.g. *although*, *but*, and *however* show that contrasting information will follow.

LANGUAGE BANK Expressions for showing contrasting information

One sentence	
Contrasting information + main information	***Although*** *Madagascar is very mountainous, it is very rich agriculturally.*
Main information + contrasting information	*Madagascar is very rich agriculturally, **although** it is very mountainous.* *It has a tropical climate **but** is dry in the south.*
Two sentences	
Main information + contrasting information	*The mountains were once covered in forest. **However**, increased agriculture has led to deforestation.*

SPEAKING Talking about countries

1 🔊 2.4 Listen and read part of the lecture again. What do you hear when there is

a a comma? _____ b a full stop? _____ **Read STUDY SKILL**

Map 2

> Map 2 shows the second of our two island states, the Philippines.
> It's very different. It is in fact made up of over 7,000 islands.
> The Philippines is situated in the Pacific Ocean in South-East Asia.
> It's got a tropical climate, so two seasons: wet and dry.

STUDY SKILL Spoken punctuation (1)

In writing, the end of a sentence is shown by a full stop. In speaking, to show the end of a sentence, the speaker's voice goes down and there is a slight pause before starting the next sentence.

In writing, a comma shows a part of a sentence or an item in a list. In speaking, to show this, the speaker pauses slightly.

2 🔊 2.5 Listen and read about Australia.

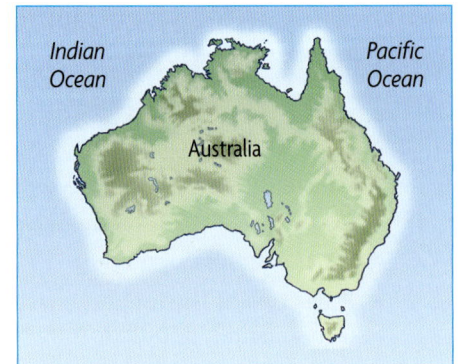

> Australia is the largest island in the world it is situated between the Pacific and Indian Oceans it has different types of climate because it is so big it is tropical in the north but has continental weather in the south the centre is very dry.

1 Add a full stop to show the end of a sentence.
2 Add a capital letter to show the start of the next sentence.
3 Add a comma to show a part of a sentence.

3 Read the paragraph in exercise 2 aloud.

4 Look at the notes for a student presentation. How are they organized?

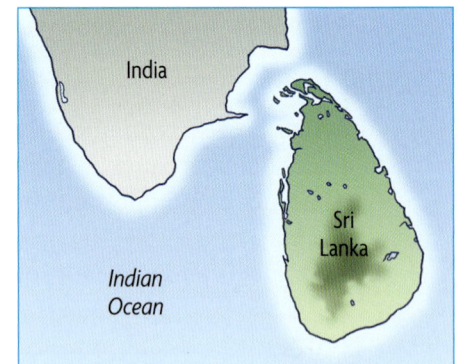

Sri Lanka

LOCATION	GEOGRAPHY	CLIMATE
• south of India, S. Asia	• low countryside	• tropical
• Indian Ocean	• mountains in south central area	• 2 monsoons = heavy rain

INDUSTRIES	AGRICULTURE
• telecoms	• very varied – tea, rice, sugar cane, rubber
• banking	
• clothing	
• tourism	

5 **Read STUDY SKILL** 🎧 2.6 Listen to two presentations. Answer the questions.

	speaker A	speaker B
1 Did the speaker use the headings in exercise 4 to organize the talk?		
2 Did the speaker signpost contrasting information?		
3 Was it clear when sentences ended?		
4 Was the presentation easy to understand? Why / Why not?		

STUDY SKILL Helping the listener (1)

It is often more difficult to listen and understand than to read and understand. Help your listeners understand you by:

- structuring your talk clearly, e.g. speaking from notes organized by headings.
- using signposts to show what type of information you are giving, e.g. for contrasting information, using *but*, *although*, etc.
- pausing and using falling intonation to show when a sentence ends.
- not speaking too quickly.

RESEARCH

1 **Read STUDY SKILL** You are going to give a short talk to your class. Research a country and write notes under the headings below.

COUNTRY _____				
LOCATION	CLIMATE	AGRICULTURE	INDUSTRIES	GEOGRAPHY

STUDY SKILL Using the Internet (1)

There are many sources of information on the Internet. A good place to start for general information is an online encyclopaedia, such as:

www.britannica.com
www.infoplease.com
www.bartleby.com
www.wikipedia.org
http://reference.allrefer.com

For more detailed information, look for articles on http://scholar.google.com

When using an online reference site, remember not all sites are reliable or accurate. Use at least two websites to check your information.

---

2 Prepare a short talk about the country you researched.

- Number the headings in the order you will talk about them.
- Include some contrasting information, with words like *but, although,* and *however*.
- Practise giving your talk. Remember to help your listeners by structuring your talk and pausing.

VOCABULARY DEVELOPMENT Synonyms

1 `Read STUDY SKILL` Match a word in column **A** with its (near) synonym in column **B**.

A	B
1 climate	a big
2 situated	b located
3 famous	c main
4 principal	d talk
5 lecture	e weather
6 large	f well-known

STUDY SKILL Avoiding repetition (1)

To make your talk more interesting, vary the words you use. Use a synonym or near synonym, e.g. *produce – manufacture*.

Read the example sentences in your dictionary to check the correct usage of the synonym, e.g.:

*The factory **produces** / **manufactures** computer chips.* ✓
*The factory **produces** a lot of waste.* ✓
*The factory **manufactures** a lot of waste.* ✗

2 Replace the words in **bold** with a word from the box.

> illustration   resulted in   states   discussing   wealthy

1 Switzerland is a very **rich** country.
2 Many **countries** need to import food.
3 Mining **led to** deforestation.
4 Singapore is a good **example** of a successful island state.
5 This week we will be **talking about** population figures for each country.

Stress on nouns and verbs

3 Look at the sentences below. Are the underlined words nouns or verbs?

1 The main <u>produce</u> is coffee.
2 Coffee factories <u>produce</u> a lot of waste.

4 🎵 2.7 Listen to the sentences in exercise 3. Mark the stress on the underlined words. `Read STUDY SKILL`

5 🎵 2.8 Listen to the words. Are they nouns (N) or verbs (V)?

1 a ___ b ___   4 a ___ b ___
2 a ___ b ___   5 a ___ b ___
3 a ___ b ___

STUDY SKILL Word stress (2)

Some two-syllable words can be both nouns and verbs, e.g. *a produce, to produce*. Often the stress changes.

- For many two-syllable nouns, the stress is on the first syllable: *produce* /ˈprɒdjuːs/
- For many two-syllable verbs, the stress is on the second syllable: *produce* /prəˈdjuːs/

6 🎵 2.9 Read the sentences aloud with the correct stress. Listen and check your answers.

1 Companies cannot import without an import licence.
2 The group will present its findings tomorrow.
3 The students gave their professor a present when he retired.
4 The secretary made a record of the meeting.
5 If you wish to record this lecture, please do so.
6 Singapore exports a lot of electronic equipment.
7 Two of the main exports from Madagascar are vanilla and coffee.

export

record

import

7 Work with a partner. Ask and answer the questions.

1 Do you do a lot of research for your studies / work?
2 Are you making progress in your English?
3 How do you record new vocabulary?
4 What academic subject do you like best?

REVIEW

1 Look at the map. Complete the sentences.

1 Japan consists of _____ main islands.

2 The biggest island is called _____ .

2 🔊 2.10 Listen to the introduction to a lecture about Japan. Tick the areas the lecturer will talk about.

1 Where Japan is and the weather ☐
2 The food grown and produced ☐
3 The population ☐
4 The main industries ☐

3 🔊 2.11 Listen to the talk. Make notes under headings based on the topics in exercise 2.

JAPAN

LOCATION & CLIMATE	AGRICULTURE	MAIN INDUSTRIES
Asia	_____	_____
_____	_____	_____
_____	_____	_____
_____	_____	_____

4 Read a summary of the lecture on Japan. Replace the words in bold with a synonym from the box on the right.

automobile   principal   rich   situated

> Japan is [1]**located** in north-east Asia. Agriculture is not the [2]**main** industry, but rice and sugar beet are grown. Japan is a [3]**wealthy** country principally because of its electronic and [4]**car** industries.

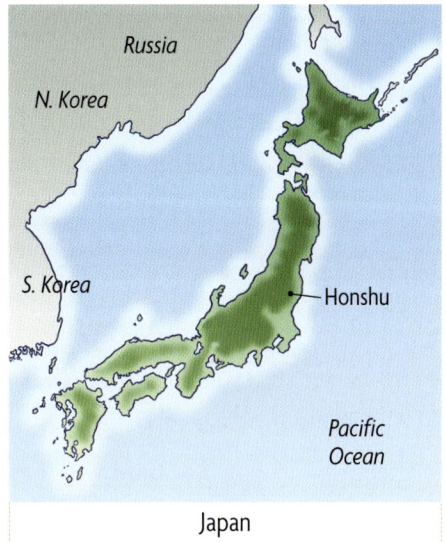

5 Read the paragraph about Jamaica below. Add:
- full stops at the end of sentences
- capital letters at the start of sentences
- commas in lists and to show parts of sentences.

> Jamaica is an island in the Caribbean Sea south of Cuba it generally has a tropical climate but the mountainous interior is more temperate agriculture is an important part of Jamaica's economy sugar cane bananas coffee citrus yams and vegetables are all grown on this small island

6 Read the paragraph about Jamaica aloud. Pause for commas, and pause and use falling intonation for the end of sentences.

🔊 2.12 Listen and check your answers.

7 Read more about Jamaica. Add words from the box.

although   but   however

> [1]_____ Jamaica exports a lot of agricultural products, tourism is its main industry. [2]_____ , recently the number of tourists has decreased. This has hurt the economy, [3]_____ the government hopes that tourism will improve again as the global economy grows.

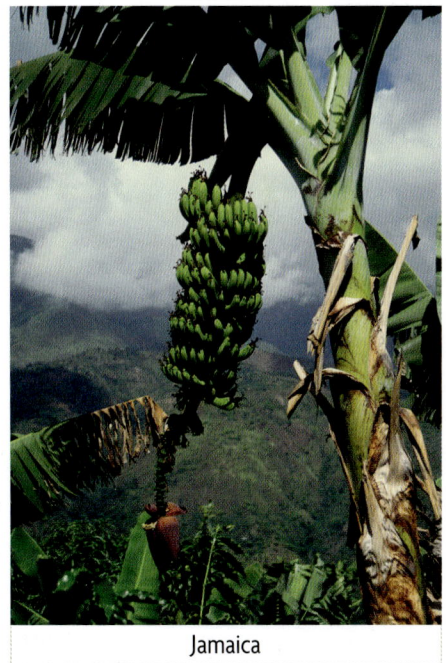

🔊 2.13 Listen and check your answers, then read the paragraph aloud.

Russia

N. Korea

S. Korea

Honshu

Pacific Ocean

Japan

Jamaica

3 Careers in the media

LISTENING SKILLS Taking notes (2) • Recognizing signposts (2)
SPEAKING SKILLS Spoken punctuation (2) • Sentence stress • Helping the listener (2)
VOCABULARY DEVELOPMENT Collocations (1) and (2)

LISTENING Two journalists

1 Work with a partner. Discuss what skills and qualities are needed to be:

- a journalist
- a scientist
- a news photographer

A journalist needs to be able to write clearly.

2 🔊 3.1 Listen to Mari Kaplan's talk on 'A career in science journalism'. Number topics a–c in the order Mari talks about them.

a ☐ Why she chose this job   b ☐ What skills she needs   c ☐ What she does

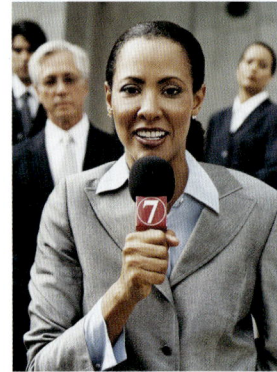

Mari Kaplan

STUDY SKILL Taking notes (2)

Taking notes as you listen helps you remember important information. Use a mind map to show how information is linked.

Degree in journalism — Qualifications

Degree in English

NEWSPAPER EDITOR

Writing articles — Tasks and responsibilities — Choosing illustrations

Correcting writing

Selecting articles

Creative — Skills and qualities

Organized — Precise

---

3 **Read STUDY SKILL** 🔊 3.1 Listen again and complete the notes.

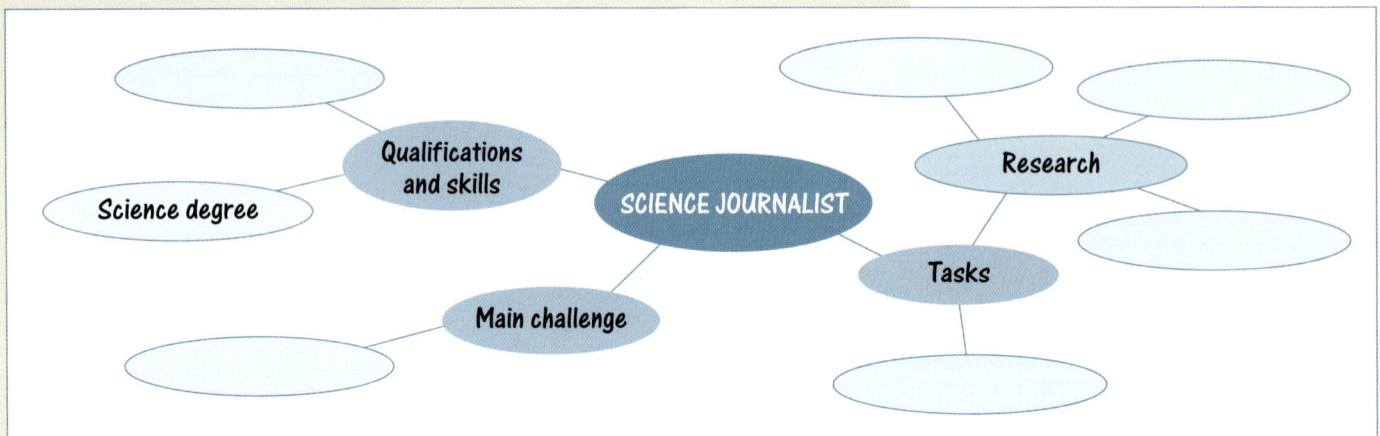

Qualifications and skills — SCIENCE JOURNALIST

Science degree

Research

Tasks

Main challenge

Signposting

4 🎧 3.2 Listen to part of a podcast interview with a TV news presenter, Ahmed Hamid. Ahmed is talking about how he started his career. Answer the questions. Discuss your answers with a partner.

1 Has Ahmed always been a news presenter?
2 Does he enjoy it?

5 🎧 3.2 Listen to Ahmed again and answer the questions.

1 What job did Ahmed do first?
2 Why didn't he want to be a newsreader?
3 What job did he first do on TV?
4 Why does the job suit him?
5 What other skills do TV newsreaders need?

6 **Read STUDY SKILL** 🎧 3.3 Listen and complete the sentences with a suitable reason or example phrase.

1 I didn't think about being a presenter _____ I wasn't very self-confident.
2 Apparently, I sound honest and serious. _____ the producer suggested more TV work to me.
3 There are a few qualities that are necessary. _____ sometimes you need to be calm.
4 Well, many things can go wrong, _____ a guest being late.
5 Sometimes you have to announce bad news, _____ a serious accident or disaster.
6 Most readers will be non-scientists. _____ we have to write in a clear and simple way.
7 I've got the science background _____ my degree in Chemistry.

Ahmed Hamid, TV news presenter

> **STUDY SKILL**
> **Recognizing signposts (2)**
>
> Remember to listen for signposts that tell you the type of information that will follow.
>
> - *Because, because of* (+ noun), and *that's why* are followed by a reason or consequence
> - *For example, for instance,* and *such as* are followed by an example / examples
>
> Recognizing these signposts will help you understand the information you need.

7 🎧 3.4 Listen to the first part of sentences 1–7 and match them with a suitable second part a–g.

1 ☑ f _____	a a lot of space is sold for advertising.
2 ☐ _____	b the Internet or academic journals.
3 ☐ _____	c an accident on the motorway.
4 ☐ _____	d she studied graphic design.
5 ☐ _____	e sports or nature pictures.
6 ☐ _____	f he hadn't enjoyed science at school.
7 ☐ _____	g business and international news.

8 🎧 3.4 Listen again and write the first part of the sentences in exercise 7.

9 Work with a partner. Complete the sentences with your own ideas.

1 I wouldn't like to be a journalist because _____ .
2 It's easy to find information today because of _____ .
3 There are a few jobs I would like to do, such as _____ .
4 It's not easy to get a job these days. For this reason, _____ .
5 There are parts of a newspaper I never read, for example, _____ .
6 Some TV programmes I really enjoy, for instance _____ .
7 I like to keep in contact with my friends and family. That's why _____ .

SPEAKING Talking about jobs and studies

1 Discuss the questions with a partner.

    1 Do you want to be a journalist?

    2 What do you want to do?

2 🔊 3.5 Listen to the questions. What does the speaker's voice do at the end of the questions?

Read STUDY SKILL Practise saying the questions with the correct intonation.

> ### STUDY SKILL Spoken punctuation (2)
>
> In *yes / no* questions (closed questions that have the answer *yes* or *no*) the intonation usually rises at the end of the question.
>
> *Did you want to present the news yourself?*
>
> In *wh-* questions (open questions which begin with a question word, e.g. *why / what / when*) the intonation often rises and then falls at the end of the sentence.
>
> *Why is that important?*

3 🔊 3.6 Listen to sentences 1–8. Are they *wh-* or *yes / no* questions? Complete the first column below.

Question type

1	yes / no	Do you have any experience?
2	_____	_____
3	_____	_____
4	_____	_____
5	_____	_____
6	_____	_____
7	_____	_____
8	_____	_____

4 🔊 3.6 Listen again and write the questions in exercise 3 in the second column.

5 Practise saying the questions with the correct rising or falling intonation.

6 **Read STUDY SKILL** 🔊 3.7 Listen and underline the stressed words.

    1 I'm going to write my essay tonight.

    2 The café doesn't open till 10.

    3 Do you have any free time this afternoon?

    4 He doesn't have any experience.

    5 I think he'll enjoy the new challenge.

    6 When's she starting the job?

> ### STUDY SKILL Sentence stress
>
> In a sentence, the important words are stressed, that is, they have more emphasis so that they are clearer. Auxiliary words, e.g. *do, am, would* and contractions, e.g. *I'd, you're* are unstressed, and are less clear. They often have the schwa /ə/ sound.
>
> *I'd <u>like</u> to go to that <u>lecture</u>.* /aɪd ˈlaɪk tə gaʊ tə ðæt ˈlektʃə/
>
> *Does <u>class</u> start at <u>10.00</u>?* /dʌz ˈklɑːs stɑːt ət ˈtenˀ/
>
> Saying sentences with the correct stress makes your speaking clearer.

7 Underline the stressed words in the paragraph about a graphic designer. Work with a partner. Take turns to read the paragraph aloud.

> Graphic designers of magazines decide how magazines should look. They choose the colours, the photos, the illustrations and the fonts, and decide the layout of the magazine. That's why they have to be creative and have good visual communication skills. They also need to have good technical skills because they use design software programs such as Adobe® Photoshop. Finally, they should be well organized so they can complete their work in time.

🎧 3.8 Listen and check your answers.

8 You are going to listen to Kalim talking about his studies. Tick the topics from the list you think he will talk about.

- ☐ subjects he is studying
- ☐ where he lives
- ☐ reasons for choosing subjects
- ☐ sports
- ☐ future job
- ☐ holiday jobs

9 🎧 3.9 Listen and compare what Kalim says with your answers to exercise 8.

10 🎧 3.9 Listen again and complete the five questions you hear.
1 So _____ ?
2 Is _____ ?
3 And why _____ ?
4 And what _____ ?
5 Why _____ ?

11 **Read STUDY SKILL** Work with a partner. Talk about your studies. Ask and answer the questions in exercise 10. Use the expressions from the Language Bank to give reasons and examples.

A magazine

Oxfordshire
Limited Edition
incorporating **Intuition**
May 2011

Shell-shocked – an Oxford artist celebrates the sea

STUDY SKILL Helping the listener (2)

You can help your listeners understand you by:
- structuring your talk clearly, e.g. speaking from notes organized by a mind map.
- using signposts to show what type of information you are giving, e.g. for giving a reason, use *because, that's why,* etc.
- using rising or falling intonation for questions.
- stressing the important content words.

LANGUAGE BANK Expressions for giving reasons and examples

Consequences and reasons
That's why (+ clause)
People want to know the news when it happens. That's why they check the news sites on the Internet.

For this reason, (+ clause)
Many employers only hire people with experience. For this reason, it can be difficult to find your first job.

Because (+ clause)
Fewer people buy newspapers today because they can find the news for free on the Internet.

Because of (+ noun)
The speaker was difficult to understand because of her accent.

Examples
For example (+ clause)
I listen to some programmes on the radio, for example discussions and documentaries.

For instance (+ clause)
Several people work together to produce an article, for instance the writer, the editor, and the graphic designer.

Such as (+ noun)
Certain TV programmes, such as cooking competitions and game shows, are very popular at the moment.

VOCABULARY DEVELOPMENT
Verb and noun collocations

1 **Read STUDY SKILL** Underline the nouns that go with the verbs in bold.

1 Ming will **introduce** the speaker at the beginning of the lecture.
2 Ana has to **attend** a lot of meetings every week.
3 The lecturer **explained** the complex idea in a simple way.
4 It took several hours to **find** all the information that was necessary.
5 I'm going to **give** my seminar paper next week.

2 Match a verb 1–5 with a noun a–e.

1	☐ find	a	a conference
2	☐ give	b	on TV
3	☐ appear	c	a programme
4	☐ attend	d	a solution
5	☐ produce	e	a talk

3 Complete the sentences, using the verbs from exercise 2 in the correct form.

1 Over a thousand people _____ the conference last month.
2 Keiko _____ a good solution to her transport problem – a bicycle.
3 The radio programme was _____ in Sydney.
4 The visiting professor will _____ a talk on her research.
5 He never wanted to _____ on TV.

4 🔊 3.10 Listen and check your answers. Underline the stressed words.

5 **Read STUDY SKILL** Choose the correct noun from the box to go with the verbs.

| TV   a lecture   an article   a programme   a conference |

1	to present to announce _____ to produce	4	to attend to give _____ to cancel
2	to write to read _____ to edit	5	to attend to organize _____ to cancel
3	to appear on to watch _____ to turn on / off		

6 Complete the collocations with *do* or *make*.

1	_____ a project	6	_____ money
2	_____ your homework	7	_____ a phone call
3	_____ an announcement	8	_____ an exercise
4	_____ a speech	9	_____ a decision
5	_____ research	10	_____ a mistake

7 Complete the questions with a suitable verb and noun collocation from exercise 6. Work with a partner and ask and answer the questions. Remember to use the correct intonation.

1 When do you usually _____ ?
2 How do you feel when you _____ in English in front of a group of people?
3 Would you like to _____ at a university in the future?
4 Do you find it easy to _____ in English?

STUDY SKILL Collocations (1)

Verbs often go together with certain nouns. These are called collocations.
to present the news
to explain an idea

The verb and the noun have equal stress.

Using collocations makes your English sound more natural.

STUDY SKILL Collocations (2)

Some nouns go together with several verbs:
to listen to
to be on   *the radio*
to switch on

Similarly, some verbs go with several nouns:

to attend   *a conference*
a meeting
a college
a lecture

Recording all these collocations helps you expand your vocabulary.

REVIEW

1 You are going to listen to an online producer talking about his job. Tick the responsibilities and skills you think he has.

- ☐ organizing a website
- ☐ writing all articles on a website
- ☐ editing
- ☐ giving technical support
- ☐ using good communication skills
- ☐ IT skills
- ☐ managing content

🎧 3.11 Listen and check your answers.

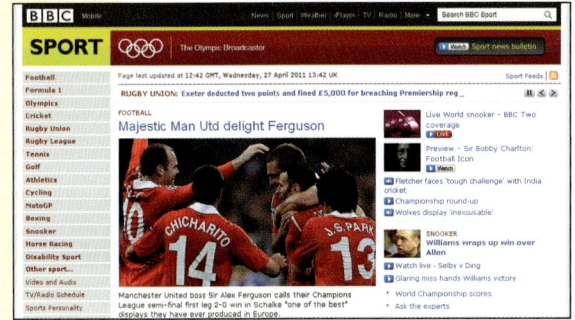

2 🎧 3.11 Listen again and complete the mind map.

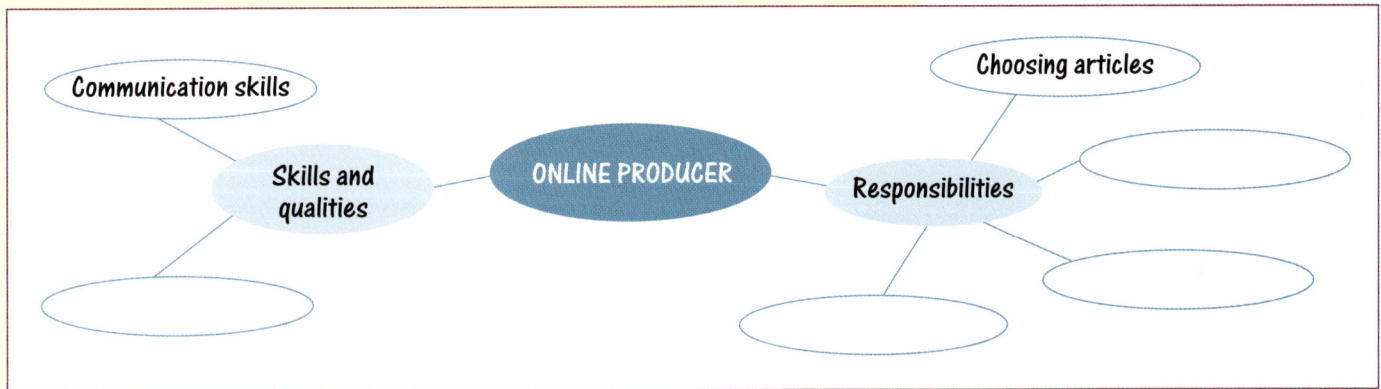

Communication skills — Skills and qualities — ONLINE PRODUCER — Responsibilities — Choosing articles

3 Match the beginnings of the sentences with a suitable word or phrase from the middle, and an ending.

1 Good communication skills are essential,	because	a lack of space.
2 I decide on the organization of the site, and	because of	b the news, are updated every two hours.
3 I don't need to be an IT expert,	for example,	c the technical creation of the website is done by IT specialists.
4 Some sections of the site,	that's why	d I need good design skills.
5 We have to keep the articles short	such as	e it's necessary to be able to write well.

🎧 3.12 Listen and check your answers.

4 Complete the questions about being an online producer. Use the question words in the box.

who	why	which	what	are

1 _____ kind of skills are needed?
2 _____ are good design skills important?
3 _____ is responsible for the technical creation of the website?
4 _____ section is updated every two hours?
5 _____ short articles necessary? Why?

5 Work with a partner. Take turns to ask and answer the questions, using the correct intonation.

4 Innovations from nature

LISTENING SKILLS Using visuals (1) and (2) • Listening for detail (1)
SPEAKING SKILLS Defining and describing objects • Helping the listener (3) and (4)
RESEARCH Using the Internet (2)
VOCABULARY DEVELOPMENT Register (1) • Multi-word verbs

LISTENING Biomimicry

1 Work with a partner. Look at the dictionary entries. Discuss what you understand by 'biomimicry'.

2 Look at Figures 1 and 2. Discuss the questions with a partner.
   1 How do the shoes close?
   2 What is sticking to the denim material?
   3 How do they stick there?

> **bio-** /ˈbaɪəʊ/ *prefix* (in nouns, adjectives and adverbs) connected with living things or human life: *biology ◇ biodegradable*

> **mimic²** /ˈmɪmɪk/ *noun* [C] a person who can copy sb's behaviour, movements, voice, etc. in an amusing way ▶ **mimicry** /ˈmɪmɪkri/ *noun* [U]

Biomimicry: an introduction – how nature has inspired inventions

seeds

hooks

Figure 1

loops

hooks

Figure 2

3 🔊 4.1 Listen to a talk on biomimicry. Work with a partner. Discuss what you think the main topics of the talk are.

4 **Read STUDY SKILL** 🔊 4.1 Listen again and use Figures 1–2 to answer the questions.
   1 When did George de Mestral go for a walk in the countryside?
   2 What did he notice after his walk?
   3 How long did it take for de Mestral to invent Velcro?
   4 What material is Velcro made of?
   5 How does Velcro stick together?
   6 What happens when you pull Velcro open?
   7 What is Velcro used for?

> **STUDY SKILL** Using visuals (1)
>
> New or important words are often presented in labelled pictures and diagrams in a talk. Study these diagrams and pictures while you listen to help you understand.

5 Match words 1–4 with definitions a–d.

1	hook	a	small hard part of a plant, from which a new plant can grow
2	loop	b	to close or join two parts of something
3	fasten	c	a curved piece of metal, plastic, etc. that is used for hanging something on or catching fish
4	seed	d	a curved or round shape, made by a line curving round and joining or crossing itself

6 `Read STUDY SKILL` Look at Figures 3 and 4 and label them with the words in the box.

| surface | blood vessels | cut | hairs |

| fibres | resin | hole |

Biomimicry

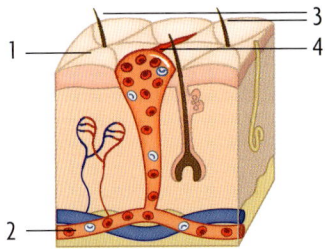

Figure 3: A cross-section through skin

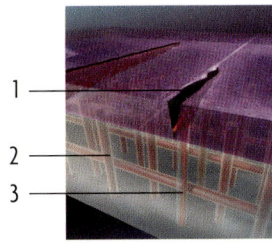

Figure 4: Self-healing plastic

4.2 Listen to a radio programme on other examples of biomimicry and check your answers.

7 4.2 Listen again and complete the sentences.

1 You can see the _____ of the skin at the top, with a few _____ coming through.
2 At the bottom, there are red and blue _____ .
3 Special blood cells move from the _____ to the _____ .
4 These cells _____ the bleeding and _____ the healing, or repairing process.
5 These fibres, which contain _____ , go horizontally and vertically through the material.

8 `Read STUDY SKILL` 4.3 Listen to the extracts and complete the sentences which rephrase the words in bold.

1 This is the material that **fastens**, or _____ things.
2 He noticed that the seeds stuck **repeatedly**, so he could remove the seed and stick _____ .
3 When the loops and hooks are separated, they produce a **characteristic ripping sound**. This is _____ tearing.
4 What happens when you cut yourself? Your body **heals**, or _____ .

9 4.4 Complete the sentences with a word or phrase in the box. Listen and compare your answers.

| These are | This is | This | those that | or |

1 Scientists are studying spider silk. _____ the material that spiders make.
2 The silk is made up of polymers. _____ long chains of connected molecules.
3 Lizards can walk up walls. How do they manage to adhere to, _____ stick to the wall?
4 Energy-efficient processes, _____ use less energy, are necessary today.
5 Many people talk about sustainable development. _____ aims to protect the environment for the future.

STUDY SKILLS Using visuals (2)

While you listen to a lecture or presentation, draw pictures or diagrams and label them. This will help you remember important information and new vocabulary.

STUDY SKILL
Listening for detail (1)

In presentations and lectures, speakers often repeat or rephrase important information. If you miss the information you need, or don't understand something, it is important to continue listening for any repetition or explanation, e.g.

I'd like to talk about self-healing plastics. ***These*** *are plastic materials that can heal or repair themselves.*

SPEAKING Describing objects

1 🔊 4.5 Listen to a student describing a gadget she has. Look at Figures 5–7 and tick the one she is talking about.

2 `Read STUDY SKILL` There are five mistakes in the description of the object below. Look at Figure 7 and correct the mistakes.

> It's a really useful object. It's made of metal and it's small so it's quite light. It has a lot of faces and each one is pentagonal in shape, in other words, it has four sides. In the middle of each face there are two points for putting a plug into. Then there's a cable which is plugged into a phone. It's called an e-ball multi-plug adaptor and it's used to adapt plugs from electronic devices to an electrical supply. It's great and everyone should have one!

🔊 4.5 Listen again and check.

STUDY SKILL Defining and describing objects

If you can't remember the word for an object, define or describe it.

- Use words such as *object, thing, machine, material, device*, e.g. *... an object that ...*
- Give a description, e.g. *It's pentagonal in shape. It's made of plastic.*
- Describe its purpose, with *for + -ing*, e.g. *It's for putting a plug into* or *to + verb*, e.g. *It's used to connect a lot of plugs.*
- Use relative pronouns, such as *which* or *that* (informal), e.g. *There's a cable which is plugged into the wall.*

3 Choose an object and write a description of it. Work with a partner. Take turns to read your descriptions and guess what the objects are.

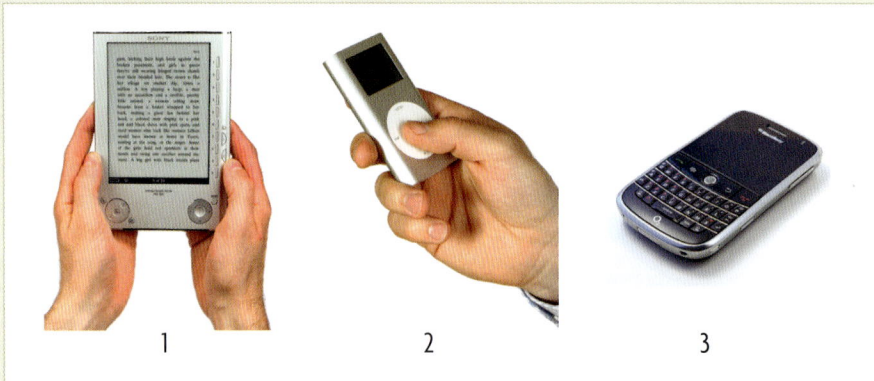

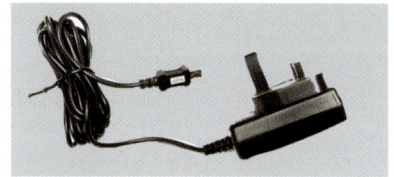

Figure 5 ☐

Figure 6 ☐

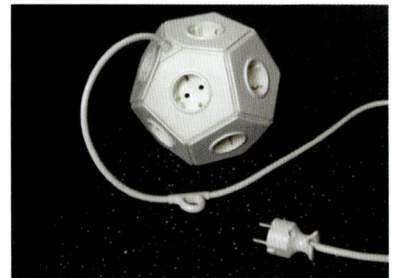

Figure 7 ☐

4 You have three minutes to prepare a one-minute talk on an object. Answer the questions below to make notes. If you can't remember the word for something, define or describe it.

What is the object?	What does it look like?	What is it used for?	Why do you use it?
•	•	•	•
•	•	•	•
•	•	•	•

5 Work with a partner. Take turns to give and listen to each other's talks.

Structuring a talk

6 **Read STUDY SKILL** 🔊 4.6 Listen and complete the introduction to a talk.

> ¹_____ how nature has inspired architecture.
> ²_____ to it – ³_____ a
> description of a natural construction which keeps a constant temperature
> and ⁴_____, how architects have copied this system
> and built a high-rise building with a similar cooling system.

7 Complete the sentences taken from a talk with expressions from the Language Bank.

> ¹_____ a piece of technology that has made my life
> much easier – the credit card. ²_____ – firstly, a short
> history, ³_____ , the advantages and disadvantages of
> a credit card, and ⁴_____ , how it affects my life. If you
> ⁵_____ , you can see one of the first credit cards ever
> made. That is the end of part three. So, ⁶_____ , you
> can see how important a credit card is today.

8 **Read STUDY SKILL** 🔊 4.8 Listen and mark the pauses (/) in the sentences.
1 When a hole forms in the surface of the material, the resin moves to the hole and blocks it, or closes it.
2 This material can be used to cover the surface of different machines, like aeroplanes, and so improve their safety.

9 🔊 4.9 Listen and read the paragraph. Mark the pauses (/). Work with a partner. Take turns to read the paragraph aloud.

> Swimmers and other athletes are always trying to swim faster, using less
> energy. To do this, they must wear clothes which produce very little friction,
> or resistance, when they move through the air or water. Scientists who
> design these clothes have studied some of the fastest fish in the sea, sharks.
> They have copied the skins of these animals and invented a material which
> reduces friction. The result is that swimmers can swim even faster and be
> more energy efficient.

RESEARCH

1 **Read STUDY SKILL** You are going to give a two-minute talk about a piece of technology or a process.
1 Choose a piece of technology to talk about.
2 Find some information about it.
3 Find a diagram or picture of it.
4 Write notes on your talk.
5 Use expressions from the Language Bank.

2 Give your talk, describing your object and pausing where necessary.

STUDY SKILL
Helping the listener (3)

Help listeners understand your talk by structuring it clearly. Use expressions to show:
- the beginning, middle, and end of a talk
- the visuals you are referring to

LANGUAGE BANK
Expressions for structuring talks

Beginnings and endings
I'd like to talk about …
My talk today is about …
There are (two / three) parts to it: …
Firstly, … Secondly…, Finally, …
First of all, …
To conclude / To sum up …

Referring to visuals
As you can see in the picture, …
The first / second / next slide shows …
Look at Figure 2.
If you look at the diagram, you can see …
This slide / picture / diagram shows …

STUDY SKILL
Helping the listener (4)

In longer sentences, words are grouped together and said in phrases to make the sentences easier to understand, e.g.:
🔊 4.7

There are two parts to it /– first of all, / a description of a natural construction / which keeps a constant temperature / and secondly, / how architects have copied this system / and built a high-rise building / with a similar cooling system.

STUDY SKILL
Using the Internet (2)

Images can be found on many websites, e.g.:
http://images.google.com/
http://www.picsearch.com/

Always give the source of any photograph you use with a complete reference, e.g.:
http://en.wikipedia.org/wiki/Velcro (29/11/11)

VOCABULARY DEVELOPMENT   Informal or formal?

1 **Read STUDY SKILL** Underline the more formal word.

1 adhere / stick
2 thing / object
3 invent / make
4 get / obtain
5 illustrations / pictures
6 prevent / stop

STUDY SKILL Register (1)

The register of language is the type of language you use, whether formal or informal. In an academic situation use formal language. In a more relaxed situation use informal language e.g.:

*All students will be able to **obtain** their results from the exams office.* (F)
*When did you **get** the results?* (I)

The register you use depends on the context or situation.

2 Underline the informal word or expression in the sentences which is inappropriate. Replace with a formal word or expression.

1 Scientists are inspired by lots of aspects of nature.
2 The professor thought the exam results were great.
3 The students were advised to watch a documentary on TV.
4 It is not OK to cancel an appointment at the last moment.
5 Schools are concerned about how much exercise kids take.
6 The lecture was sort of interesting.

🔊 4.10 Listen and check your answers.

3 Replace the formal word or expression in bold with an informal one from the box.

made	stuck	like	much better	get here	thing

1 When did the speaker **arrive**?
2 The ring tone on his mobile is **similar to** mine.
3 We **produced** a model of the Formula 1 car in the lab.
4 This **object** is really great.
5 We **attached** the pieces of wood together.
6 My tutor said the second draft of my essay was **a great improvement**.

adhere stick
get   obtain
prevent   stop

4 **Read STUDY SKILL** Replace the formal verb in bold with an informal multi-word verb from the box in its correct form.

get to	go down	go over	think about	carry on	find out	work out	put off

1 The scientists **discovered** why the fish could swim so fast.
2 When he **arrived at** the library, he started writing his report.
3 I **reviewed** all my lecture notes before I wrote my essay.
4 **Continue** with the discussion until you agree.
5 Food prices **fell** by 5% last month.
6 Musical people can usually **solve** logical puzzles easily.
7 Don't decide until you have **considered** everything.
8 The meeting was **postponed** until next week.

STUDY SKILL Multi-word verbs

A multi-word verb is a verb combined with a preposition or adverb (or both) which can sometimes give a new meaning. These verbs are often informal, e.g.:

*The two parts of the Velcro can be **pulled apart** many times.*
*De Mestro **took** the seeds **off** his coat.*

5 Complete the questions with a multi-word verb from exercise 4 in its correct form. Work with a partner. Ask and answer the questions.

1 What time did you _____ college today?
2 Are you good at _____ mathematical problems?
3 Have you ever _____ changing your job/your studies?
4 Do you often _____ doing work until the last moment?
5 When you finish this course, will you _____ with your studies?
6 Do you always _____ your notes before an exam?

REVIEW

1 You are going to listen to part of a lecture on how insects have inspired the building of an office block. Match the titles with the illustrations, using a dictionary to help you.

> a **An office complex and shopping centre** ___
> b **A cross-section through a termite mound** ___

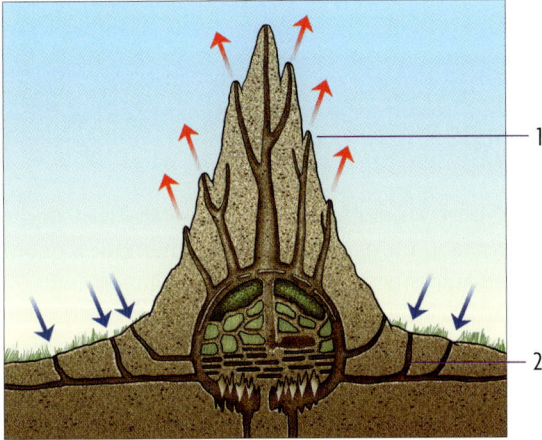

Figure 1

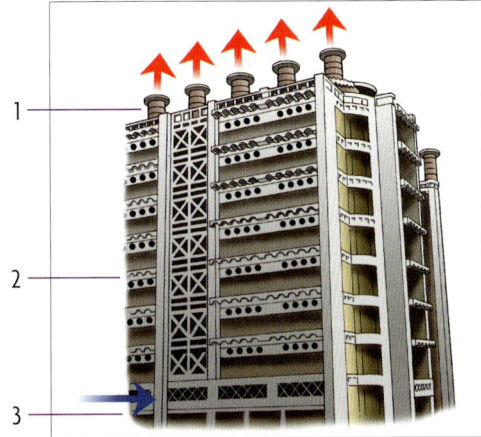

Figure 2

2 Label Figures 1 and 2 with the words in the box.

> chimneys   vents   concrete arches   chimneys   vents

🔊 4.11 Listen and check your answers.

3 🔊 4.11 Listen again and answer the questions.
1 Where is the Eastgate office complex and shopping centre?
2 Why is the Eastgate Centre unusual?
3 Why do termites open and close the vents in their mounds?
4 How does warm air escape from the Eastgate Centre?
5 What is the purpose of the concrete arches?
6 Compared to other buildings, how much energy is used in the Eastgate Centre?

4 Replace the formal word or expression in bold with an informal one from the box. Work with a partner. Ask and answer the questions.

> get out   stay   start   left out   asking

1 Have you ever **omitted** a question in an exam? Why?
2 What time does your first lecture **commence** in the morning?
3 How late do you **remain** at university or college in the evenings?
4 If you were **enquiring** about student accommodation, who would you contact?
5 If you were stuck in a lift, what would you do to **escape**?

5 Conversations

LISTENING SKILLS Listening for detail (2) • Distinguishing speakers • Distinguishing levels of formality
SPEAKING SKILLS Conversational topics • Keeping a conversation going (1) and (2)
VOCABULARY DEVELOPMENT Word building (1) and (2)

LISTENING Welcome to the first day

1 Read the notice for the conference. Which degrees in the list are *multi-disciplinary*? Compare your ideas with a partner.

- ☐ M.A. European Law & Technology
- ☐ B.Sc. Pure & Applied Chemistry
- ☐ B.A. Business Administration & Japanese
- ☐ M.Sc. Mechanical Engineering & Social Sciences

What are the advantages or disadvantages of multi-disciplinary degrees?

2 You are going to listen to the welcome speech on the first day. Tick the information you expect to hear.

- ☐ a welcome to participants
- ☐ hotel arrangements
- ☐ introductions
- ☐ lunch menu
- ☐ room details
- ☐ time details
- ☐ history of the conference

  🎧 5.1 Listen and check your answers.

3 Brainstorm four or five words associated with subjects 1–4. Compare your ideas with a partner.

1 Nursing Studies *hospital*   3 Engineering
2 Law   4 Environmental Studies

4 **Read STUDY SKILL** 🎧 5.1 Work in groups of four. Listen again and note the information you need.

Student **A**   You are interested in Engineering.
Student **B**   You are interested in Environmental Studies.
Student **C**   You are interested in Law.
Student **D**   You are interested in Nursing Studies.

International Conference on Multi-Disciplinary Studies

In the past, students went to University and studied one subject, for example Pure Mathematics, or two related subjects such as French Language and Literature. However, today we need graduates with a wider understanding of the world. This is why many universities are now offering degrees in two subjects, for example European Law and Technology. This approach to education is known as multi-disciplinary and the Organization of Multi-Disciplinary Studies (OMDS) aims to encourage this development by events such as our conference this week.

Day 1 Programme

9–9.30 Welcome Speech (Dr Felipe Castillo-Fiera, Chair, Organizing Committee) Main Hall

STUDY SKILL Listening for detail (2)

Before listening, think about what information you need. Listen for the key words and associated words. Don't listen for information you do not need. Selecting *what* to listen for will help you focus on the relevant information.

student	topic / subject of talk	room	time
A Engineering			
B Environmental Studies			
C Law			
D Nursing Studies			

5 🎧 5.2 Listen to part of each of the four lectures. Which lecture would students A–D listen to?

1 ___   2 ___   3 ___   4 ___

Which words helped you decide?

Who is speaking?

6 Look at the photograph. Answer the questions.

1 Where are the people?
2 What do you think they are talking about?

7 **Read STUDY SKILL** 🎧 5.3 Listen to the start of a conversation. Answer the questions.

1 How many people are talking in total?
2 How many are men? How many are women?

> **STUDY SKILL** Distinguishing speakers
>
> It can be difficult to understand if there are several people speaking. Listen for different accents and tones. This will help you decide who is speaking, and to understand what they are saying.

8 🎧 5.4 Listen to the rest of the conversation. Match each speaker 1–4 with their opinions a–d about Dr Smart's lecture.

speaker	opinion
1 ☐ Tom O'Farrell (first man)	a brilliant
2 ☐ Louisa Parker (first woman)	b excellent
3 ☐ Rebecca Fong (second woman)	c interesting
4 ☐ Richard West (second man)	d one of the best

9 **Read STUDY SKILL** 🎧 5.5 Listen to the whole conversation. Answer the questions.

1 Which of the speakers know each other?
2 Which person is a stranger?
3 Is the conversation formal, informal, or neutral? How do you know?

10 🎧 5.6 Listen to three conversations. Are the speakers friends (F), a mixture of teachers and students (TS), or strangers (S)?

1 ___   2 ___   3 ___

11 🎧 5.6 Listen again. Complete the conversations.

1 **A** _____ , what did you think of Dr Smart's talk?
  B _____ . Um, I thought it was very interesting.

2 **C** _____
  D _____
  C _____ so far?

3 **E** That was fascinating, wasn't it?
  F _____ , but I _____ in the middle.
  G _____ , but the handout _____ .

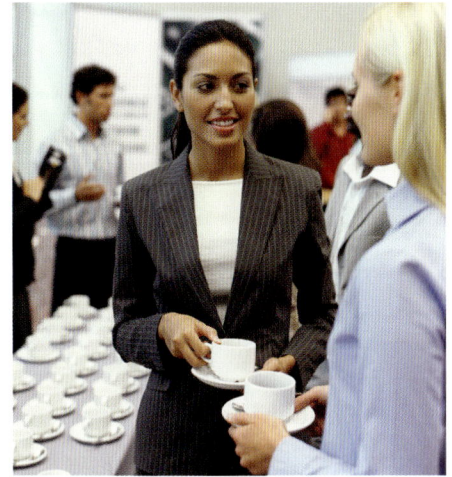

> **STUDY SKILL**
> Distinguishing levels of formality
>
> Listen to *how* people speak to each other and what level of formality they use. This will help you understand the relationship between them, e.g. work colleagues, teachers and students, students, or strangers.

SPEAKING Making conversation

1 Work with a partner. Would you discuss these topics with a friend (F), a stranger (S), or both (FS)?

- the weather   ____
- your salary / income   ____
- politics   ____
- a place, e.g. the city you are in / where you study / work   ____
- work / studies   ____
- family   ____

2 **Read STUDY SKILL** 🔊 5.7 Listen to four conversations. Are the speakers friends (F) or strangers (S)?

Conversation 1 ____   Conversation 3 ____

Conversation 2 ____   Conversation 4 ____

STUDY SKILL Conversational topics

How you speak depends on who you are speaking to and the topic you talk about. With people you don't know, talk about neutral topics, e.g. the weather, places, work, your studies.

Topics for conversation vary in different countries. For example, in many countries it would not be correct to ask about someone's salary. It is important to find out and respect these cultural 'rules'.

3 **Read STUDY SKILL** 🔊 5.7 Read and listen to the conversations again. Underline the examples of returning questions.

1 **A** Hi, Lucy! How's your family?
  B Hello, Sally. They're fine, thanks. <u>And yours?</u>
  A Yes, well, thanks. Are you going …

2 **A** It's a great city for a conference, isn't it?
  B Yes, it is. Is this the first time you've been here?
  A No, actually, I know the city quite well. What about you?
  B This is the first time …

3 **A** I'm from Chicago.
  B Really! Me, too. Where exactly?
  A Hyde Park district, near the university. And you?
  A I'm quite close to you. I've got an apartment …

4 **A** I've finished my essay. How about you?
  B Another five minutes. Will you wait for me?
  A Yeah, sure. I'll just …

STUDY SKILL Keeping a conversation going (1)

To keep a conversation going, invite the other person to speak by:
- asking a new question, e.g. *Is this the first time you've been here?*
- asking for further, more detailed, information, e.g. *Where exactly?*
- returning a question, e.g. *And you / yours?, What / How about you?*

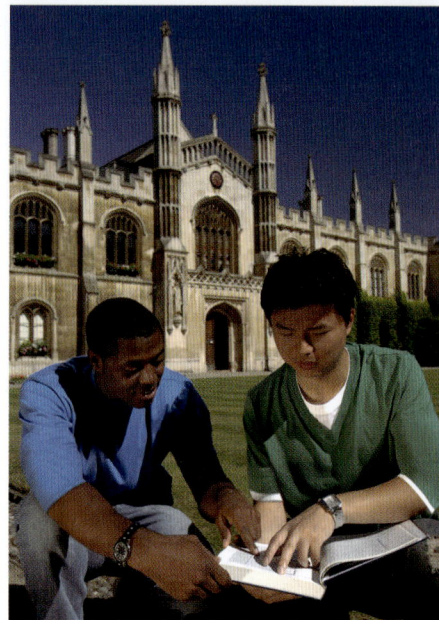

4 🔊 5.8 Read and listen to the conversation. Work with a partner. Take turns to keep a conversation going. Student **A** Start the conversation. Student **B** Keep the conversation going by asking questions and for more information.

Student **A** OK, that's it. I think I'll stop now and have a break. What about you?

Student **B** Yes, I think I will too. Are you going for lunch now?

Student **A** Yes, I am – what are you going to do?

> Are you from here?
>
> Are you enjoying the course?
>
> What did you think of the lecture?
>
> What are you doing at the weekend?

5 🔊 5.9 Read and listen. Complete the conversation with the words in the box.

study habits   and   really   Leyburn

A I had an interesting time this weekend.

B ¹_____ ? What did you do?

A I went on a study trip to Leyburn.

B ²_____ ?

A Yeah, it's a small coastal town in the north.

B Oh, ³_____ ?

A Well, it was fascinating. We did a survey of study habits.

B ⁴_____ ?

A Yeah, study habits. It was amazing what we discovered about …

6 **Read STUDY SKILL** Work with a partner. Practise the conversation in exercise 5. Use the correct intonation.

STUDY SKILL Keeping a conversation going (2)

To keep a conversation going, show interest in what the speaker is saying. Use: 🔊 5.10

- *Really?* with rising intonation

- *And?* with rising intonation

- repetition of a key word with rising intonation, e.g. *Leyburn?*

You can express stronger interest by increasing the level your voice rises:

- *Really?* and *Really?*

---

7 Work with a partner. Take turns to have two conversations, using the instructions given.

1 **A** Start the conversation. Tell your partner about something you did at the weekend.

   B Show interest and ask for more information.

   A Continue the conversation.

2 **B** Start the conversation. Tell your partner about something you have seen in the news.

   A Show interest and ask for more information.

   B Continue the conversation.

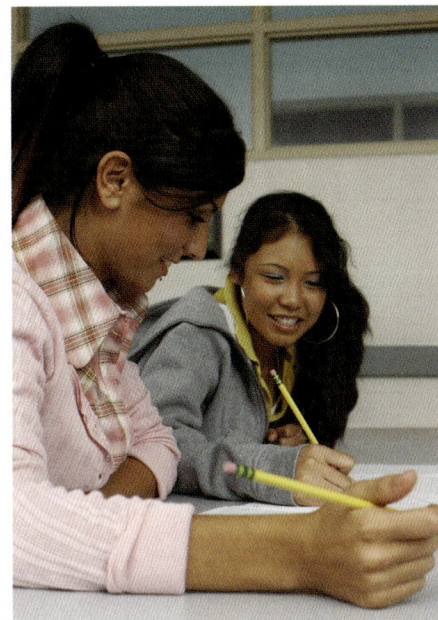

VOCABULARY DEVELOPMENT Suffixes

1 **Read STUDY SKILL** 5.11 Listen to the words. Underline the main stress. Do you notice any patterns?

1 discussion   introduction   conversation
2 biology   archaeology   anthropology
3 medical   musical   physical

2 Underline the stress on the words. Practise saying the words aloud.

1 administration   4 technology   7 electrical
2 education   5 geology   8 mechanical
3 pronunciation   6 zoology   9 economical

5.12 Listen and check your answers.

3 5.13 Listen and mark the stress on the words in bold. Practise saying the sentences aloud.

1 The **government** is increasing tax on fuel.
2 We are looking into the **development** of a new multi-disciplinary course in Arabic and American Studies.
3 Thank you for that very interesting talk on the **environment**.
4 This morning's lecture is on the early history of **capitalism**.
5 As a teacher, you must not show **favouritism** in the classroom.
6 I know many of you are interested in a career in **journalism.**
7 The **friendliness** of the island people is well known.
8 The accident was caused by the driver's **carelessness**.
9 **Blindness** can be caused by bacteria in rivers and lakes.
10 Young children have the **ability** to learn languages easily.
11 The local **community** will benefit from the new sports centre.
12 It is important that biological **diversity**, that is, the range of animals and plants, is maintained.

Prefixes

4 **Read STUDY SKILL** Add a prefix from the box to the word in brackets to complete the sentences.

anti	bi	micro	multi	post

1 A _____ (organism) is a very tiny living creature.
2 A _____ (-doctorate) student is someone who continues to study after they have a Ph.D.
3 An _____ (-theft) alarm is a device in a car that makes a loud noise if someone tries to steal the car.
4 A _____ (national) organization is one that works in many different countries.
5 A _____ (annual) event is one that happens twice in one year.

5 5.14 Listen and check your answers. Listen again. Mark the stress on the words. Practise saying the sentences aloud.

STUDY SKILL Word building (1)

Suffixes are added to the end of a word and tell you the part of speech of that word.

- Common noun endings are: *-ion, -ment, -logy, -ness, -ism, -ity*
- Common adjective endings are: *-ful, -ical, -al, -able*
- For these suffixes: *-ion, -logy, -ical* the main word stress is on the preceding syllable, e.g. *discussion* /dɪˈskʌʃn/

For other suffixes, use a dictionary to find the main stress in the word you need.

-ion

-ology

-ment

STUDY SKILL Word building (2)

Prefixes are added to the beginning of a word and change the meaning of the word. For example, a book about the life of a person is a *biography*. A book about the life of a person written by the person is an *autobiography*.

Use your dictionary to check the stress pattern.

REVIEW

1 Put the key words and phrases under the correct heading in the table.

> accountancy   buildings   design   human resources   Internet   microchip   profit
> production   skyscrapers   social networking   urban planning   world wide web

Business Management	IT (Information Technology)	Architecture

2 5.15 Listen to the introduction to three lectures.

  a Number the subjects from exercise 1 1–3 in the order you hear them.
    Business Management _____   IT _____   Architecture _____
  b Listen again and tick the key words and phrases in exercise 1 that are used.

3 5.16 Listen to three conversations. How many speakers are there in each conversation?

  1 ___   2 ___   3 ___

4 5.17 Listen to two conversations. Answer the questions.

  a What is the topic of conversation?
  b Are the speakers friends (F) or strangers (S)?

	Topic	(F)/(S)
Conversation 1		
Conversation 2		

5 5.18 Read and listen to the conversation. Complete the gaps with words and phrases that keep the conversation going.

  A Is this your first term?
  B Yes, it is. ¹_____ ?
  A Yes! And I'm having problems finding my lecture room!
  B What ²_____ is that?
  A Archaeology 101.
  B ³_____ ?
  A Yes. ⁴_____ ?
  B I'm studying Archaeology, too!

6 Work with a partner. Take turns to have a conversation using the prompts.

Student A	Student B
1 Tell your partner about your plans for the evening, weekend, or holidays.	2 Show interest and ask for more information.
3 Give more information and ask about your partner's plans.	4 Tell your partner your plans.
5 Show interest.	

6 Food science

LISTENING SKILLS Listening for gist (2) • Taking notes (3) • Interpreting meaning
SPEAKING SKILLS Helping the listener (5) • Checking understanding
VOCABULARY DEVELOPMENT Collocations (3)

LISTENING Functional foods

1 Work with a partner. Look at the photos and discuss the questions.

1 What is the name of the food in each picture?
2 Why do people eat these types of food?

2 6.1 Listen to three extracts from a lecture and list the foods in the order you hear about them. Which key words helped you?

1 _____ 2 _____ 3 _____

3 Read STUDY SKILL 6.1 Listen again and tick the attitude of the lecturer. What helped you find the answers?

	unsure	enthusiastic	certain
Extract 1	☐	☐	☐
Extract 2	☐	☐	☐
Extract 3	☐	☐	☐

4 6.3 Listen to the first part of the lecture and tick the correct answer for each question.

1 What is 'functional food'?
  a food that gives nutrition ☐   b food that gives extra benefits ☐
2 What would **not** be added to make functional food?
  a bacteria ☐   b sugar ☐
3 What is iodine?
  a a salt ☐   b a mineral ☐
4 What happens to young children if they do not have enough iodine?
  a They can have low intelligence. ☐
  b They can have problems moving. ☐
5 Does iodine occur naturally in salt?
  a yes ☐   b no ☐

5 Read STUDY SKILL 6.3 Listen again and answer the questions. Write the figures only.

1 When was the name 'functional food' invented? _____
2 How many people in the world don't have enough iodine? _____
3 When was iodine added to salt in Tanzania? _____
4 What percentage of the population of Tanzania did not have enough iodine in their diet in the 1990s? _____
5 What percentage of children now has normal levels of iodine?
  _____

a   b   c

STUDY SKILL Listening for gist (2)

Recognizing the attitude of the speaker, or how they think and feel about something, can help you understand a talk or lecture. Listen for the intonation of the voice and words that express different attitudes, e.g.:

 6.2
- **enthusiastic**
  This is very important.
  It's a wonderful invention.
- **certain**
  I'm sure.
  This has been clearly shown.
- **unsure**
  There is some truth in that, but ...
  Maybe.

STUDY SKILL Taking notes (3)

When taking notes of numbers, write the figures, not the words.

You hear *sixty per cent*. Write *60%*.

Numbers are often repeated in a lecture. If you don't hear or understand a number, continue to listen for the repeated information.

25 per cent, that's a quarter.
One in two people, that's fifty per cent.

Facts and speculation

6 🔊 6.4 Listen to the second part of the lecture. Tick the statements that are true.

1 Omega 3s are beneficial to health. ☐
2 Omega 3s are made by the body. ☐
3 They are added to foods like juice and milk. ☐
4 Probiotics are live bacteria. ☐
5 Probiotics are added to eggs. ☐

7 **Read STUDY SKILL** 🔊 6.4 Listen again and complete the sentences.

1 These are ones containing the fatty acids Omega 3s, which _____ reduce the risk of heart disease.
2 They _____ beneficial effects on other diseases, such as some cancers.
3 And, it _____ Omega 3s improve brain function in older people.
4 They _____ naturally in certain foods, like some fish.
5 However, now food manufacturers _____ Omega 3s to common foods, such as fruit juice, eggs, and milk.
6 Probiotics _____ foods like yogurts and yogurt drinks.
7 _____ think that they help the body fight diseases.
8 Indeed there is some evidence that probiotics _____ attack certain infections.

STUDY SKILL   Interpreting meaning

Speakers express facts (what happened) and speculate (guess).

Facts are true statements.
42% of the population in Tanzania were lacking iodine.

Speculation is uncertain. It can be expressed with:
- a modal verb, e.g. *Probiotics **may** attack certain infections.*
- words and phrases, e.g. *This functional food has **probably** saved hundreds of lives.*
- verbs, e.g. *Scientists **think** that they help the body fight diseases.*

It is important to distinguish between facts and speculation.

---

8 Work with a partner. Are the statements in exercise 7 expressed as fact or speculation?

9 Change the factual sentences into speculation, using the words in brackets.

1 Taking vitamin pills is not always good for you. (might)
   Taking vitamin pills might not always be good for you.
2 A poor diet causes brain damage. (possibly)
3 Eating fish is good for the brain. (Some people believe that)
4 Yogurts that contain live bacteria are better for you. (may)
5 Superfoods such as blueberries help prevent cancer. (Experts claim that)
6 A little chocolate every day is not bad for you. (probably)
7 Too much fat in your food causes heart disease. (can)
8 Not enough physical exercise is bad for your heart. (Doctors think that)
9 A stressful lifestyle is a cause of cancer. (It is possible that)

🔊 6.5 Listen and check your answers.

10 Work with a partner. Do you agree with the statements?

SPEAKING Expressing approximations

1 **Read STUDY SKILL** ⦿ 6.6 Listen to the pairs of sentences with approximations and write in the appropriate number.

394	62	406	489	58	510

1 ___ people attended the lecture.
2 ___ people attended the lecture.
3 The equipment cost € ___ .
4 The equipment cost € ___ .
5 The lecture lasted for ___ minutes.
6 The lecture lasted for ___ minutes.

STUDY SKILL Helping the listener (5)

Help your listeners understand numbers by:
- repeating or rephrasing them
- using approximations

2 ⦿ 6.6 Listen again and check your answers.

3 Express the numbers in sentences 1–8 as approximations in as many different ways as possible. Use expressions from the Language Bank.

1 The report contained <u>67 pages</u>.

| almost 70 pages |
| about 70 pages |
| under 70 pages |

2 Prices increased by 2.1% last month.
3 A return ticket costs €19.
4 1.984 grams of salt was added to one litre of liquid.
5 The computer was in constant use for 6 hours 57 minutes.
6 The library was closed for three weeks five days.
7 397 people have enrolled for the conference.
8 The cost of repairing the building was €300,130.

Compare your answers with a partner. Practise saying the approximations aloud.

LANGUAGE BANK Expressions for giving approximations

around / about
e.g. *The semester finishes in around / about three weeks. (20 days)*

approximately (Formal)
e.g. *The results showed that approximately 95% of the children were now out of danger. (95.4%)*

almost / nearly
e.g. *The study took almost / nearly 12 weeks. (11 weeks and five days)*

(just) more than / (just) over
e.g. *There are more than / over 20 places in the seminar room. (23 places)*

(just) less than / (just) under
e.g. *A new computer costs less than / under €800. (€786)*

---

4 Work with a partner. Ask and answer these questions. Give approximate numbers.

1 How many students attend your college / school / university?
2 How many people live in your city?
3 What is the average temperature in your country in July?
4 How much does a kilo of coffee cost in your country?
5 How long does your journey to college / school / university / work / take in the morning?

Checking understanding

5 You are going to listen to part of a seminar on bacteriophages. These are viruses that kill bacteria. Discuss the questions in small groups.

1 What happens to fresh fruit and meat after a few days?
2 Why is some food kept in the fridge?
3 Why do you think food companies add bacteriophages to food?

6 🎧 6.7 Listen and complete the notes. Check your answers to the questions in exercise 5.

> ### Bacteriophages (viruses that kill bacteria)
>
> Date discovered _____
>
> Advantages   1 _____
>
>   2 _____
>
> Added to food by _____
>
> Safety? _____

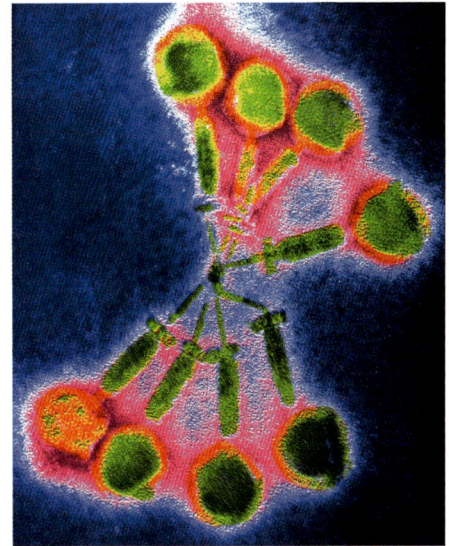

Bacteriophages

7 🎧 6.7 Listen again and tick the expressions in the Language Bank that you hear.

> **LANGUAGE BANK** Expressions for checking understanding
>
> | **Speaker** | **Listener** |
> | --- | --- |
> | Asking the listener questions | Asking for repetition or clarification |
> | *Do you know what I mean (by ...)?* | *Could you repeat that name / word, please?* |
> | *Is that clear / OK / alright?* | *Could you explain ...?* |
> | Asking the listener for questions | Checking understanding by repeating |
> | *Do you have any (other) questions?* | *So what you're saying is ...* |
> | *Would you like to ask anything?* | *So that's ...* |

8 **Read STUDY SKILL** Work with a partner. Take turns to use your notes about bacteriophages and the expressions in the Language Bank to have a conversation, following the instructions.

Student A	Student B
1 Say what bacteriophages are.	
	2 Ask for repetition.
3 Repeat what you said.	
4 Give the two advantages of bacteriophages.	
	5 Check your understanding by repeating what Student **A** has said.
6 Say yes.	
7 Ask if Student **B** has any questions.	
	8 Ask a question about the safety of bacteriophages.
9 Answer the question.	

> **STUDY SKILL**
> Checking understanding
>
> It's important to make sure any information you are giving or receiving is communicated correctly.
>
> When speaking:
> - check the listener understands.
> - ask if the listener has any questions.
>
> When listening:
> - ask for clarification or repetition.
> - check you have understood by repeating the information to the speaker.

VOCABULARY DEVELOPMENT
Adjective and noun collocations

1 **Read STUDY SKILL** Underline the adjectives and nouns that go together in the sentences.

1 Eating fruit and vegetables every day has a <u>beneficial effect</u> on your health.
2 A lack of iodine can cause low intelligence in children.
3 There was a slight increase in the price of milk last month.
4 Adding iodine has produced an enormous improvement.
5 Doctors recommend everyone has a balanced diet.

2 Complete the sentences with the correct adjective.

1 Supermarkets offer a _____ choice of food.
   a long   b wide   c big

2 Only a _____ amount of salt should be eaten every day.
   a little   b light   c small

3 Some people have to live on a _____ diet.
   a weak   b poor   c little

4 Doctors have reported a _____ improvement in the general health of people.
   a wide   b narrow   c slight

5 There is some simple advice on how to have a _____ lifestyle.
   a wide   b beneficial   c healthy

3 Cross out the adjective that does not go with the noun.

1 healthy balanced strong poor	diet	2 a wide a weak a good a limited	choice	3 fresh tinned dried junk	fruit
4 fast fresh junk wide	food	5 poor serious minor major	illness	6 gentle physical regular weak	exercise

4 6.8 Complete the sentences with a word from the box. Listen and check your answers.

> beneficial   high   stressful   small   fresh   physical

1 Do you eat _____ fruit every day? What do you eat?
2 What do you do to manage a _____ lifestyle?
3 Do you think regular _____ exercise is important? What exercise do you take?
4 Do you believe functional foods have _____ effects on health? Give some examples.
5 Do you think a ___ amount of chocolate is good for you? Why / Why not?
6 Can certain foods help you develop ___ intelligence? Give some examples.

5 Work in small groups and discuss the questions in exercise 4.

balanced diet

fresh food

slight improvement

high intelligence

REVIEW

1 6.9 Listen to an interview about functional foods. Is Dr Reinhardt certain, unsure, or enthusiastic?

2 6.9 Listen again and answer the questions.
   1 Which foods are not as good as functional foods?
   2 Give two reasons why extra minerals or vitamins are added to foods.
   3 Name two situations when people might need functional foods.
   4 Give three examples that show that functional foods are a growing market.

3 You are going to listen to the second part of the interview. Before you listen, tick which of the sentences you think are facts and which are speculation.

statement	fact	speculation
The market will grow.	☐	☐
Substances like Omega 3s will be developed.	☐	☐
People are concerned about their health.	☐	☐
Food companies are developing new foods.	☐	☐
Some new foods protect people from diseases.	☐	☐
The future of functional foods is exciting.	☐	☐

6.10 Listen and check your answers.

4 Look at some Recommended Daily Allowance (RDA) values for an adult.

Calories	2000
Protein	50g
Carbohydrates	300g
Fat	65g
Fibre	25g

You are going to compare two breakfast cereals in Figures 1 and 2. Work with a partner. Student **A**, talk about the cereal Healthy Way and Student **B**, talk about the cereal Good Balance. Follow the instructions.

Student A	Student B
1 Choose one ingredient in Healthy Way, say how much of it there is, and speculate about why it is important.	
	2 Ask for repetition of the amount.
3 Repeat what you said.	
	4 Give similar information about Good Balance and speculate about why it is important.
5 Clarify what Student **B** said by repeating it.	
	6 Confirm or correct what Student **A** said. Add another piece of information about Good Balance.
7 Ask a question about what Student **B** said.	
	8 Answer the question.

5 Discuss with your partner which cereal you think is healthier. Give reasons.

Healthy Way Cereal
with added calcium for stronger teeth & bones

For every 100g

Calories	418
Protein	9.8g
Carbohydrates	73.1g
Fat	8.5g
Fibre	7g

Figure 1

GOOD BALANCE Cereal

For every 100g

Calories	449
Protein	8g
Carbohydrates	57g
Fat	16g
Fibre	18g

with added Omega 3s which help to protect from disease

Figure 2

7 Great lives

LISTENING SKILLS Taking notes (4) • Listening for detail (3)
SPEAKING SKILLS Presentations • Spoken punctuation (3) • Giving opinions, agreeing, and disagreeing
VOCABULARY DEVELOPMENT Register (2) and (3)

LISTENING Heroes and heroines

1 Look at the photos from a website about Elizabeth Garrett Anderson. Work with a partner and discuss the questions.

1 Which century was Elizabeth Garrett Anderson born in?
a the 18th century   b the 19th century   c the 20th century

2 What was her job?
a a teacher   b a poet   c a doctor

2 🔊 7.1 Listen to the introduction to a podcast about Garrett Anderson called *Heroes*. Check your answers in exercise 1.

3 You are going to listen to the rest of the podcast about Elizabeth Garrett Anderson. Tick the information you expect to hear.

☐ achievements   ☐ qualifications   ☐ character   ☐ birth
☐ death   ☐ education   ☐ family

🔊 7.2 Listen and check your ideas.

4 **Read STUDY SKILL** 🔊 7.2 Listen again and complete the headings and notes.

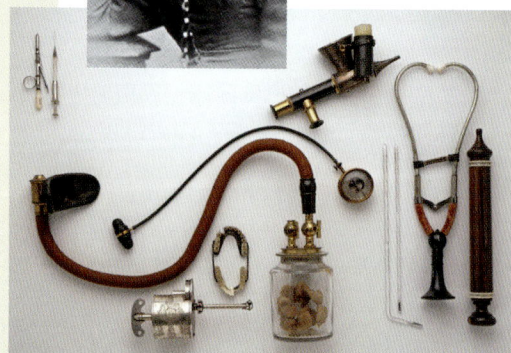

ELIZABETH GARRETT ANDERSON

1 _____
     born _____
     one of _____ children
2 Education / Qualifications
     _____ school
     enrolled as _____ student
     1865 Society of _____ (= chemists)
     learnt _____
     medical degree at University of _____
3 Problems
     impossible for _____ to study medicine
     banned from _____
4 _____
     determined, _____,
     courageous, _____
5 _____
     first woman doctor
     founded a _____ for women
     became an _____ for other women

STUDY SKILL Taking notes (4)

It is easy to miss information when you are taking notes. If you do not hear clearly the information you need:

- write down what you think you heard. Do not worry about spelling. Check the information later in a reference book or on the Internet. For example, *1865 Society of '**Apothikaris**'*. If you put this into a search engine, it says *Do you mean 'apothecaries'?*

- put a question mark to remind yourself to check the information later. For example, *born 183?*

It is important to continue listening so that you do not miss other information.

Opinions and facts

5 🔊 7.3 Listen to James, Yasmin, and Parvin discussing their heroes. Complete the table. Listen as many times as you need to.

	Alexander Fleming	Crick and Watson	Florence Nightingale
nationality		Crick – English Watson – American	
profession(s)	biologist		nurse and statistician
achievement			

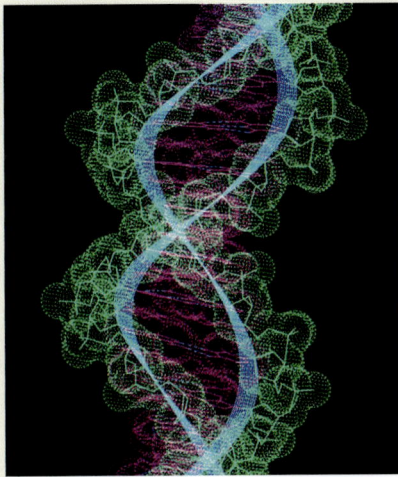

DNA helix

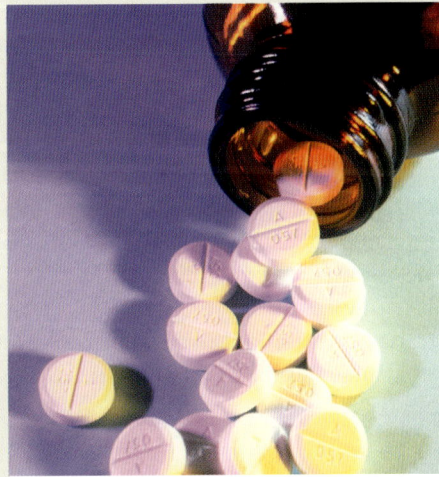

penicillin

6 🔊 7.3 Listen again. Answer the questions. Write James (J), Yasmin (Y), or Parvin (P).

1 Who thinks their grandfather is a hero? ___
2 Who thinks that Florence Nightingale is a hero? ___
3 Who thinks that Fleming is a better hero than Garrett Anderson? ___

7 Read STUDY SKILL 🔊 7.3 Listen again. Are these statements fact (F) or opinion (O)?

1 A hero is someone who has found a cure for a disease. ___
2 Penicillin has saved millions of lives. ___
3 Yasmin's grandfather is a hero. ___
4 Crick and Watson are heroes. ___
5 The discovery of DNA has changed the world of medicine. ___
6 Getting doctors and nurses to wash their hands saved thousands of lives. ___

> **STUDY SKILL** Listening for detail (3)
>
> To express opinions, speakers use phrases such as:
>
> *To my mind, ...*
> *For me, ...*
> *Personally, ...*
> *In my opinion, ...*
>
> Listening for these phrases will help you distinguish between opinions and facts.

SPEAKING My hero

1 Look at the list of professions. Which do you most admire? Compare with a partner and explain your ideas.

- engineers
- doctors
- fire fighters
- writers
- teachers

2 **Read STUDY SKILL** You are going to give a presentation on 'Why Carl von Linde is a hero.' Read the encyclopaedia entry. Underline important information.

CARL VON LINDE (1842–1934) was a German professor and engineer. He is remembered as the inventor of the first practical refrigerator or 'fridge'.

He was born in Berndorf, Germany and was the son of a clergyman. At first, he was expected to follow in his father's footsteps but, instead, he chose to study engineering in Zurich, Switzerland.

He graduated in 1864 and went on to work in a cotton-spinning plant and later in a locomotive factory. Then, in 1868, he became a lecturer and researcher in engineering at a new university in Munich. It was here that he started to work on the process of cooling, or refrigeration. In 1873, after five years of research, he built the first practical and portable compressor refrigerator.

The invention of the fridge allowed ordinary people to keep their food safe from bacteria and mould. In this way it was an invention that changed people's lives.

Von Linde married Helene Grimm in 1866, and they had six children. The 'father of refrigeration' died in Munich in 1934.

Carl von Linde

3 Make notes for your presentation, using the headings below.

WHY CARL VON LINDE IS A HERO
A Background
B Education / Qualifications
C Career
D Achievements
E Opinion

Give a one-minute presentation about von Linde.

4 7.4 Listen to a student talk about von Linde. Answer the questions.
1 Did the speaker include the same information as you?
2 Did the speaker include information you did not use?
3 Did the speaker put the information in the same order as you?
4 Which was more successful? Why?

Pausing

5 🔊 7.5 Listen and read the sentences. Add commas where the speaker pauses.

1 She was born in East London which was a very poor part of the city.
2 Madame Curie who was Polish lived most of her life in France.
3 Lancaster University where I studied was founded in 1964.

Read STUDY SKILL Practise saying the sentences above with the pauses.

> ### STUDY SKILL Spoken punctuation (3)
>
> In formal presentations, you can use complex sentences with clauses to give extra information. In writing, the extra information is put between commas in the middle of a sentence, or between a comma and a full stop at the end of a sentence. When speaking, pause to show where the clause begins and ends. This will help your listeners understand they are hearing extra information.
>
> *Carl von Linde, [pause] who invented the fridge, [pause] was originally expected to study religion.*
>
> *Von Linde invented the compressor fridge, [pause] which is a type of cooling device using oxygen.*

Agreeing and disagreeing

6 **Read STUDY SKILL** 🔊 7.6 Listen and complete the students' discussion with expressions from the Language Bank.

Student **A** Well, ¹_____ a real hero is an ordinary person who does something extraordinary. You know, like that group of blind climbers who conquered Everest. Now, they're heroes ²_____ .

Student **B** ³_____ because that's a personal act of heroism. By 'hero' I mean someone who is respected and admired for doing something that has an effect on the lives of many people.

Student **C** ⁴_____ . A hero has to be someone who has had a real impact on how we live.

Student **A** Yes, I suppose ⁵_____ . In that case, ⁶_____ I'll vote for Alexander Fleming. His discovery of penicillin has saved millions of lives.

Student **B** Yes, that's not a bad suggestion, but what about …

7 Work with a partner. Look at the table in exercise 5 on page 41. Discuss which one of the three people is a hero, using expressions from the Language Bank.

8 Prepare a short presentation.
- Choose a famous person whom you admire.
- Use the Internet or reference books to get information.
- Make notes using headings, numbers, etc.
- Use expressions to show your opinion.
- Practise giving your presentation, pausing to show the clauses which give extra information.

9 Work with a partner. Take turns to give your presentation about your hero. Discuss *which* of the two will be your joint hero. Use expressions from the Language Bank to give your opinion and to agree or disagree.

> ### STUDY SKILL Giving opinions, agreeing, and disagreeing
>
> In seminars and tutorials, you will need to express your opinion, and agree or disagree with the opinions of other people. It is especially important to be polite when you disagree.

> ### LANGUAGE BANK
> #### Expressions for discussion
>
> Giving opinions
> *In my opinion ... (F)*
> *I think / believe ...*
> *For me,*
> *It seems to me ...*
>
> Agreement
> *I quite agree* (with you). (F)
> *You're right.*
> *That's right / true.*
> *Exactly.*
>
> Disagreement
> *I'm afraid I disagree. (F)*
> *I disagree.*
> *No, that's wrong.*

VOCABULARY DEVELOPMENT Register

1 **Read STUDY SKILL** Put the phrases for disagreeing in order from 1 (the most formal) to 5 (the most informal).

a ☐ I think you could be wrong.
b ☐ I'm terribly sorry, but I don't think you're right.
c ☐ I think you're wrong.
d ☐ No, you're wrong.
e ☐ I think you could be mistaken.

🎧 7.7 Listen and check your answers.

2 Match a request 1–4 with the person they are speaking to a–d.

1 ☐ What was that?
2 ☐ Sorry, what did you say?
3 ☐ Would you mind repeating that, please?
4 ☐ Could you say that again?

a a teacher
b a fellow student
c a work colleague
d a close friend

Formal and informal verbs

3 Match a one-word verb 1–6 with a multi-word verb a–f.

1 ☐ increase
2 ☐ decrease
3 ☐ collect
4 ☐ discover
5 ☐ enter
6 ☐ omit

a come / go in
b find out
c go down
d go up
e leave out
f pick up

4 **Read STUDY SKILL** Complete the sentences with a one-word verb from exercise 3 in the correct form.

1 Last year an increasing number of young people _____ university to study Business Administration.
2 Next week we will _____ who exactly was responsible for the breakthrough.
3 It is hoped that food prices will _____ again this month.
4 Students can _____ their marked essays from the department secretary.
5 He _____ important information about his research in the article.
6 We hope to _____ the numbers of overseas students studying here.

5 Read a student's report to a tutorial group. Replace the multi-word verbs in bold with a one-word verb in the correct form.

eradicate	argue	suggest	discover	study	choose

Lee and I ¹**fell out** initially about our choice of hero. I had chosen Marie Curie, but Lee had ²**come up with** Jonas Salk. We discussed it for some time and then decided to ³**look into** the effects of both people's work more deeply. Then I ⁴**found out** how Jonas Salk had developed the vaccine for polio and that this vaccine, and a later one, ⁵**killed off** polio around the world and saved millions of lives. So, finally I also ⁶**went for** Salk.

🎧 7.8 Listen and check your answers.

STUDY SKILL Register (2)

The register used in speaking (words and grammar, and tone of voice), depends on the relationship between the speakers. Be more formal if the person you are speaking to is:

- older
- in a higher position than you, e.g. a teacher or manager
- a stranger

It is especially important to be more formal when disagreeing, requesting, etc. Use:

- phrases such as *I'm sorry, I'm afraid, I think*
- modal verbs, e.g. *could*
- positive adjectives with *not*, e.g. *I don't think that's **right***.

If you are not sure which register to use, it is better to be more neutral or formal.

STUDY SKILL Register (3)

In formal, academic speaking and writing, it is better to use one-word verbs rather than multi-word verbs, e.g.:

*The price of coffee is expected to **increase** by 20%.* (not ~~go up~~ by 20%)

REVIEW

1 🔊 7.9 Listen to the introduction to a talk about Jonas Salk. Complete the headings 1, 2, and 3 in the notes.

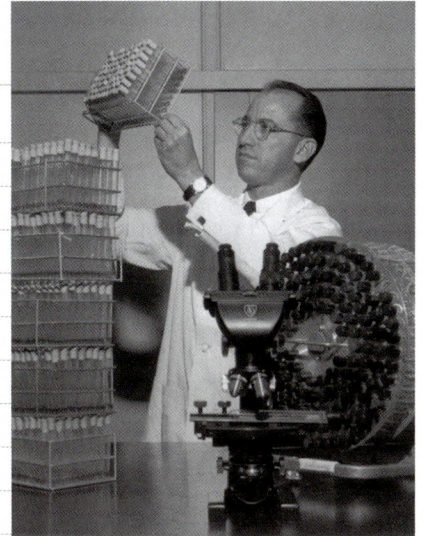

NAME: Jonas Salk   NATIONALITY: _____   PROFESSION: _____

1 _____

    1.1 born: 19___

    1.2 family: _____

    1.3 college: law then _____

2 _____

    2.1 worked w Thomas Francis Jr – a _____ to discover a _____ vaccine

    2.2 1947 head Virus _____ Lab. Univ. of _____

    2.3 19 ___ tested 1st vac. on _____ (inc. _____ and himself!)

    2.4 1955 became _____

3 _____

    3.1 _____

    3.2 _____

Jonas Salk

2 🔊 7.10 Listen to the rest of the talk and complete the notes. Check spelling and dates, if necessary, in a reference book or on the Internet.

3 🔊 7.11 Listen to a discussion about the talk. Write true (T) or false (F).

  1 Salk's polio vaccine was more widely used than Sabin's. ___
  2 Sabin's work on a polio vaccine would not have been possible without Salk's work. ___
  3 Suheir agrees with Lee's choice. ___

4 🔊 7.12 Add commas to the paragraph to show clauses. Listen and check your answers.

> Albert Sabin who was born in 1906 discovered the first oral polio vaccine. It was much easier to vaccinate people especially children by giving the vaccine on a sugar lump than injecting them with a needle. Using this vaccine which is so easy to give polio has been practically eradicated and millions of lives have been saved.

Practise reading the paragraph aloud, pausing to indicate commas.

5 Work in small groups. Look at the statements. Take turns to agree or disagree. Give an opinion or reason.

  1 Studying Engineering is more useful than studying History.
  2 Learning English is essential for a good education.
  3 The most important quality for a doctor to have is intelligence.

8 Communication

LISTENING SKILLS Understanding incomplete speech • Contractions and linking
SPEAKING SKILLS Asking questions in a survey • Register (4) • Reporting results
VOCABULARY DEVELOPMENT Modifying adjectives • Ordinary and strong adjectives

LISTENING A survey on e-communicating

1 Look at Figures 1–5. Which ways of communicating do you use the most? Compare your answers with a partner.

KEY	
1 mobile phone	3 SMS on phone
2 email	4 blog
	5 social network page

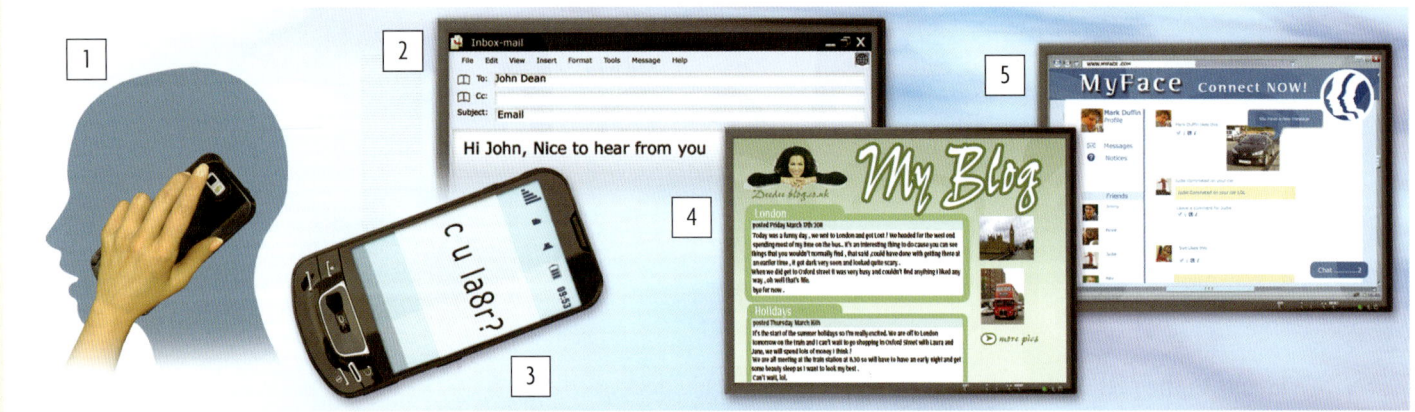

2 🔊 8.1 Listen to three extracts from a survey on the ways people communicate electronically. Tick the methods each speaker uses.

methods of communicating	speaker 1	speaker 2	speaker 3
emails			
phone calls			
SMS / texting on phone			
social networking			
blogs			

3 **Read STUDY SKILL** 🔊 8.1 Listen again. Write the exact words that correspond to the complete sentences.

1 _____ I suppose I use texts the most.
2 _____ I don't use it.
3 _____ I'm between 18 and 24 years old.
4 _____ It's a waste of time. I don't know why people use them.
5 _____ I use them all the time.
6 _____ I like my friends to know what I'm doing.

STUDY SKILL Understanding incomplete speech

In conversations, when people speak informally their speech can be incomplete.

There may be no subject in the sentence, or they may use only short phrases:
Do you use Internet access on your phone?
No, don't use it much. / Not that much (= I don't use it much.)

Speakers change how they say something, or they say the same thing in different ways:
But I suppose texting the most. Yes, I text a lot.

This can make it difficult to understand. Listen for stress on the content words, and whether the speaker rephrases what they say.

Understanding spoken English

4 8.2 Listen to three extracts from a survey about different uses of mobile phones. Decide if the statements are true (T), false (F) or not given (NG).

Speaker 1 uses her Internet connection regularly. ___
Speaker 2 uses his mobile phone for checking his emails. ___
Speaker 3 uses all of her apps. ___

5 8.2 Listen again and answer the questions.

1 What does Speaker 1 mainly use her phone for?
2 How many texts does she send and receive every day?
3 Does Speaker 2 send texts or make calls the most?
4 What does he use the Internet for?
5 Which function does Speaker 3 use the most?
6 How many apps has she got?

6 **Read STUDY SKILL** 8.3 Listen to sentences 1–6. Write the number of words you think there are in each sentence. Count contractions (e.g. *I'm*) as one word.

sentence	number of words
1	
2	
3	
4	
5	
6	

A mobile phone user

STUDY SKILL Contractions and linking

In spoken English, individual words are not always easy to understand. This can be because:

- contractions are used, e.g.:
  I don't /aɪ dəʊnt/
  I'll /aɪl/
- a word ends in a consonant sound and the next word begins with a vowel sound, so the two words are linked and not clear, e.g.:
  If it's urgent, could you tell me? /ɪfɪtsˈɜːdʒənt cʊdjəˈtelmi/

Recognizing words that are contracted or linked can help your listening comprehension.

---

7 8.3 Listen again and complete the sentences.

1 _____ a survey.
2 _____ mobile phone?
3 _____ without it.
4 _____ of apps.
5 _____ apps?
6 _____ remember.

Count the words and check your answers to exercise 6.

SPEAKING Asking questions

1 You are going to listen to an extract from a survey on Internet connections at home. Tick the words and phrases you expect to hear.

☐ choosing a computer   ☐ dial-up
☐ wireless   ☐ helpline
☐ emails   ☐ downloading
☐ speed of connection   ☐ recycling computers

🔊 8.4 Listen and check your answers.

2 **Read STUDY SKILL** 🔊 8.4 Listen again and complete the questions for the answers given.

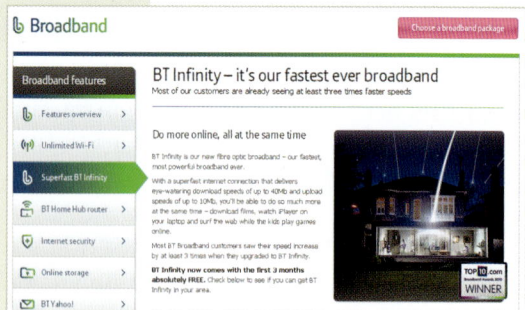

Questions		Answers
1 _____ a few questions?		OK.
2 _____ Internet at home?		Yes, I do.
3 _____ do you have?		Er, broadband.
4 _____ wireless network?		Yes, it is.
5 _____ a) very fast, b) fast, c) slow, or d) very slow?		I'd say a) very fast.
6 _____ if there's a problem with the connection?		I phone the helpline.
7 _____ a) excellent, b) very good, c) good, d) poor, or e) very poor?		b) very good.

STUDY SKILL Asking questions in a survey

The type of questions you ask depends on the information you need.

For a full answer, ask *wh-* or 'open' questions:
What do you do if there's a problem?

For specific answers, ask a *yes / no* or closed question:
Is it a wireless network?

For answers you can compare easily, ask multiple-choice questions to limit the possible answers:
Is the speed of the Internet connection: a) very fast, b) fast, c) slow, or d) very slow?

---

3 Practise the dialogue with a partner, using the correct intonation for the questions.

Speaking to strangers

4 **Read STUDY SKILL** Match the beginning of the sentences with their middle and ending.

1 Excuse me! Would you mind	for	few questions?
2 Good afternoon! May I	much for	your time.
3 Excuse me! Could you	answering	a few questions?
4 Thank you	ask you a	answering my questions.
5 Thank you very	answer	some questions for me?

🔊 8.5 Listen and check your answers. Practise saying the sentences.

STUDY SKILL Register (4)

If you need to ask for information from people you don't know, remember to use polite, formal language.

Start with an expression:
Excuse me!

Use modal verbs for a polite request:
May I ask you a few questions, please?

Thank people with a polite phrase:
Thank you very much for your help.

Reporting results

5 🔘 8.6 Listen to a report on the findings of the survey in exercise 1. Number the information in the order you hear it.

a ☐ age of people   c ☐ different types of connection
b ☐ conclusion   d ☐ number of people questioned

6 🔘 8.6 Listen again and answer the questions.

1 What was the purpose of the survey?
2 How many people were questioned?
3 How old were they?
4 What kind of connection did most people have?
5 How fast was the Internet connection for users of broadband?
6 How fast was the connection for dial-up users?
7 How did a minority of people describe the helpline service?
8 What was the conclusion of the report?

7 **Read STUDY SKILL** Prepare a report about the findings, from the survey on mobile phones, using the notes. Do not give the numbers in the Results section. Instead, use expressions from the Language Bank.

> Purpose: **to find out about use of mobile phones**
>
> Number of people interviewed: **20**
>
> Ages: **18–22**
>
> Questions: **use of mobiles, frequency of texting, calling, Internet, & other apps, etc.**
>
> Results: **20 owned mobiles**
> **16 main use – texting, (10–20 texts a day)**
> **second use – calling (average 5–10 calls a day)**
> **2 used Internet on phone for emails, general information search, & social networking**
> **Other apps used e.g. games, camera, calendar, etc**

8 Work with a partner. Take turns to give your report.

Doing a survey

9 Work in groups. You are going to carry out a survey. Your teacher will give you the topic.

1 Brainstorm the information you want to find out.
2 Write six questions to find this information, using different types of questions.
3 Ask other members of the class your questions, using the correct intonation. Remember to use polite formal phrases to start and end your questions.
4 Write down the answers. If necessary, check you understand them.
5 With other members of your group, put all the answers together. Prepare a report on your findings, using expressions from the Language Bank.
6 Present your report to the class.

broadband

dial-up

Internet

helpline

wireless

STUDY SKILL Reporting results

When reporting results or findings, give clear general information. It is not necessary to give the specific questions or individual replies. Give:

- the purpose of the survey / test / experiment
- the numbers of people involved
- the method you used, e.g. face-to-face, by telephone
- the most important results using statistical expressions, e.g. *most people*
- a conclusion

LANGUAGE BANK Expressions for reporting results

One hundred per cent
100% of the people surveyed had Internet access at home.

The majority (F)
The majority had Internet access at home.

Most people
Most people had a very fast connection.

Some
Some of the group had never used their phone to play games.

A minority (F)
A minority of people used dial-up connections.

Only ten per cent
Only ten per cent of those questioned used the helpline service.

A few
A few students called home every day.

No one
No one used their phone while driving.

On average
On average, people sent five texts a day.

VOCABULARY DEVELOPMENT Adverbs and adjectives

1 Read STUDY SKILL Underline the adverbs that modify the adjectives in the sentences.

1 The questions in the survey were very simple so the results were easy to calculate.
2 In the quiet lecture theatre the sound of the mobile phone was extremely loud.
3 Installing the new program was not very complicated so downloading the file was really fast.
4 The examination was less difficult than the students had expected.
5 The Internet connection was fairly slow.

2 Complete the scale with the adverbs from the box.

very	not very	really	extremely	fairly

weakest ←——————————————→ strongest

3 Complete the sentences about you with an adverb from exercise 2. Discuss your answers with a partner.

1 My Internet connection at home is ________ fast.
2 The signal here for my mobile phone is ________ strong.
3 Buying things on the Internet is ________ safe.
4 In my opinion, a social network is ________ useful for communicating with people.
5 I think designing a website is ________ difficult.

4 Read STUDY SKILL Rewrite the sentences using a strong adjective from the box and the adverb *absolutely*.

fascinating	perfect	enormous	impossible	freezing	terrified	exhausted

1 I was very tired. *I was absolutely exhausted.*
2 The report was very interesting.
3 Kalim found the exam very difficult.
4 The winters were very cold.
5 The arrangements for the conference were very good.
6 The lecture theatre was very big.
7 Lina was very nervous before doing her presentation.

8.7 Listen and check your answers. Practise saying the sentences aloud with the correct stress.

5 Complete the sentences with the adverb *very* or *absolutely*.

1 Wireless connections are ________ useful.
2 The results of the survey were ________ interesting.
3 The lecture was ________ fascinating.
4 Living without a mobile phone would be ________ impossible for me.
5 The seminar room was ________ small.
6 My parents were ________ delighted with my results.
7 I found the exercise ________ difficult.
8 The amount of information on the Internet is ________ enormous.

STUDY SKILL
Modifying adjectives

It is possible to make an adjective stronger or weaker by using an adverb. Use adverbs such as *not very*, *less* and *fairly* to make the adjective weaker:

It's not very important.

Use adverbs such as *very*, *really*, and *extremely* to make the adjective stronger:

It's extremely complicated.

really
extremely
absolutely
very
fairly

STUDY SKILL
Ordinary and strong adjectives

Some ordinary adjectives have a stronger equivalent:

important–essential, pleased–delighted.

Strong adjectives can be made stronger with adverbs such as *absolutely*.

It's absolutely essential.

Very is not used with strong adjectives.

Really can be used with both types of adjective.

Strong adjectives are usually stressed. When an adverb is also used both the adverb and the adjective are stressed.

REVIEW

1 8.8 You are going to listen to three students discussing some work they are preparing. Listen to the extracts and answer the questions.

	conversation 1	conversation 2	conversation 3
What is the main topic of conversation?			
What do the students agree to do?			

2 8.9 Listen to conversation 1 again and complete the sentences.

> **Student A** So, [1]_____ ideas for our presentation?
> What [2]_____ we should talk about?
> **Student B** Well, I thought we could do something on using mobile phones.
> **Student C** Not [3]_____ . What about access to the Internet?
> **Student A** What [4]_____ ?
> **Student C** I mean, where and how people access the Internet. At home, university, in parks ...
> **Student B** [5]_____ ?
> **Student C** Yes, in some cities, [6]_____ Internet in the parks.
> **Student A** Yeah, and in some cafés too. I suppose we could do that. And who pays? At home [7]_____ pay for Internet access, at university it's free, and so on.
> **Student B** Yes, OK then. [8]_____ that. Access to the Internet. We can do some research on the net.

3 Work in groups of three. Practise reading the conversation in exercise 2 aloud.

4 8.10 Listen to conversation 2 again and write the exact words that correspond to the more formal complete expressions.

> **Informal**
> 1 _____
> 2 I've found _____ about free access in different countries.
> 3 Yeah, but not _____
> 4 _____

> **Formal**
> Sorry, what did you say?
> I have found a lot of information about free access in different countries.
> Yes, but not too many slides.
> I'll send you my information by email.

5 Write four questions to ask a partner about their access to the Internet. Use the question words in the box.

> Where ...?   Why ...?   Do you...?   What kind ...?
> How much ...?   What ...?   How often ...?   Have you ...?

Where do you usually access the Internet?

6 Work with a partner. Take turns to ask and answer your questions from exercise 5.

9 Significant objects

LISTENING SKILLS Supporting an argument • Understanding words in context • Taking notes (5)
SPEAKING SKILLS Helping the listener (6) and (7)
RESEARCH Using the Internet (3)
VOCABULARY DEVELOPMENT Compound adjectives • Compound nouns

LISTENING The Lewis chess set

1 Label Figures 1–3 using the words in the box.

> a wheel   a Roman mirror   chessmen

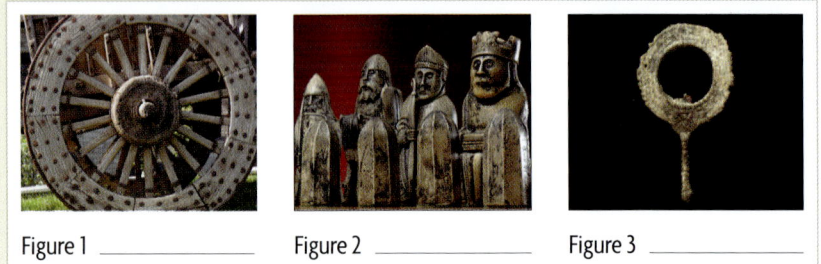

Figure 1 _____   Figure 2 _____   Figure 3 _____

2 Work with a partner. Answer the questions about the objects in exercise 1.

1 Which object has changed human history the most? How?
2 Which object has changed human history the least? Why?
3 Which object would you like to own? Why?

3 🔊 9.1 You are going to listen to a radio programme about the Lewis chessmen and the game of chess. Listen and answer the questions.

1 When were the Lewis chessmen made?   _____
2 Where did the game of chess come from?   _____

4 **Read STUDY SKILL** 🔊 9.1 Listen again and make notes on the supporting reasons why the Lewis chess set is significant.

POINT OF VIEW: The Lewis chess set is a significant historical object.	
1 a tradition of playing games	1.1 _____
2 _____	2.1 6th century India
	2.2 _____
	2.3 _____
3 _____	3.1 _____

> **STUDY SKILL**
> **Supporting an argument**
>
> In lectures, good speakers always support their argument with reasons, evidence, and examples.
>
> Listening for the supporting points will help you follow the speaker's argument, and help you decide if you agree with it or not.

5 🔊 9.2 Listen to the programme about mirrors. Mark the statements true (T), false (F), or not given (NG).

1 Glass mirrors were first made around 6000 BCE. ___
2 The earliest mirror was found in present-day Italy. ___
3 People used cosmetics for the first time in 6000 BCE. ___
4 People could see the world in two new ways with mirrors. ___
5 The first mirrors must have seemed magical. ___

6 🔊 9.2 Listen again and make notes of the supporting reasons for the speaker's point of view.

POINT OF VIEW: The mirror is _____ .	
Reason 1 _____	
Reason 2 _____	example _____
	example _____

7 Read STUDY SKILL 🎧 9.3 Listen to some descriptions of the Lewis chessmen and mirrors. Number the phrases (1) to (3) in the order you hear them.

☐ in other words ☐ that is ☐ which means

STUDY SKILL Understanding words in context

If a speaker is using words that are difficult to understand, they will often explain the vocabulary by using:

- phrases, e.g. *such as, which means, that is, or, in other words*
- a defining phrase, e.g. *Mirrors were made of **obsidian, a type of stone***.

Even if you do not understand a word or phrase at first, continue to listen for further explanations or examples.

---

8 🎧 9.3 Listen again and circle the word or phrase which is the best definition of each word.

1 carved   a decorated
           b marked
           c cut

2 convex   a flat
           b curved out
           c curved in

3 graves   a places where soldiers live
           b places where dead bodies were buried
           c places where leaders go

9 🎧 9.4 Listen to a description of the Hoxne pepper pot. Complete the sentences with the missing words. Do not worry about spelling.

1 A _____ is the top half of a person.
2 A _____ is a type of dress.
3 _____ are valuable stones.
4 Someone who is _____ has a lot of money.

10 Read STUDY SKILL 🎧 9.5 Listen to the whole talk. Complete the notes, using words, phrases, abbreviations, and symbols.

SIGNIFICANT OBJECT: The Hoxne pepper pot		
Reasons: 1 _____		
2 _____		
Background: found in _____		
Date: hidden _____ ∵ _____		
Other items: _____ coins:	_____ gold and silver items :	
_____ solid gold	_____ silver spoons	
_____ silver	_____ pepper pots	

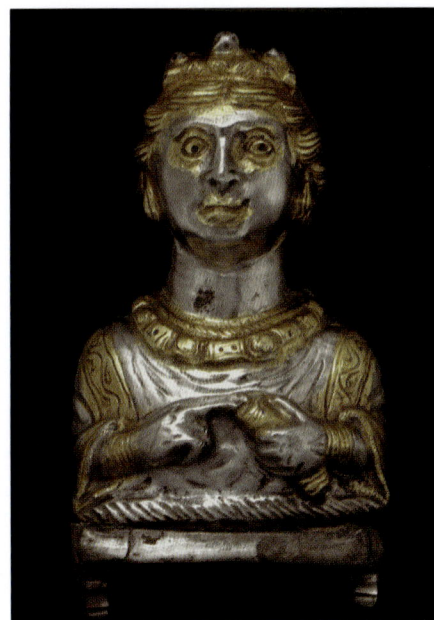

The Hoxne pepper pot

STUDY SKILL Taking notes (5)

In a lecture you often have to take a lot of notes. To do this quickly and effectively:

- write down only key words and phrases, not complete sentences
- use abbreviations, *e.g.* (*for example*), *i.e.* (*that is*), etc.
- use symbols, e.g.   − under / less than   + over / more than   → leads to / to   ∴ therefore   ∵ because
- use your own shorthand, for example, *prob* instead of *probably*, *wd* and *cd* instead of *would* and *could*, etc.

SPEAKING Machines

1 **Read STUDY SKILL** Read the notes on the Singer Sewing Machine and check the meanings of any new words in a dictionary. Rephrase, explain, or give examples of this vocabulary, using words and phrases in the Study Skills box.

The Singer Sewing Machine company was founded, that is, started, in 1851.

OBJECT: SINGER SEWING MACHINE　　　USA mid 19th cent.
HISTORY:　SSM company founded 1851
1st domestic machine 1857
1870　170,000+ machines sold
1880　½ million+ machines sold
1913　3 million+ machines sold
SIGNIFICANCE:
① revolutionized domestic life for women
e.g. before SM 10 hours to make a dress / with SM 1 hour
1.1　women had more free time
1.2　women did extra sewing to make money
② machines → mass production of clothes in factories
2.1　more women went out to work
2.2　many women suffered poor conditions and low wages

The Singer Sewing Machine

STUDY SKILL Helping the listener (6)

When you present information in a seminar or tutorial, it is likely that you will use specialized vocabulary. Help your listeners by rephrasing, explaining it, or giving examples of it:

Rephrasing	Explaining	Giving examples
that is	*this / which means*	*for example*
in other words		*such as*
that is to say		

2 **Read STUDY SKILL** Give a one-minute presentation on the historical significance of the sewing machine, using the notes in exercise 1 and the explanations of the vocabulary.

LANGUAGE BANK Expressions for supporting an argument

Listing	Adding	Giving evidence	Giving reasons	Giving examples
Firstly,	*Furthermore,*	*This shows ...*	*It is ... because (of)*	*For example,*
Secondly,	*Moreover,*	*This proves ...*	*... is why it is ...*	
Lastly,	*In addition,*			

STUDY SKILL
Helping the listener (7)

When you present an argument, it is important to support it with reasons, evidence, or examples. Use words or phrases from the Language Bank to introduce your supporting arguments.

3 🎧 9.6 Listen to a presentation about the sewing machine. Answer the questions.

1　Did the speaker use the same information as you?
2　What words or phrases did the speaker explain?
3　What phrases did the speaker use to explain the words?

RESEARCH

1 Read STUDY SKILL Use the Internet to find which museums display these objects:

1 the Mona Lisa _____

2 Kismet, the world's first sociable robot _____

3 the sarcophagus of Tutankhamun _____

4 'Sue', the most complete skeleton
   of Tyrannosaurus Rex _____

5 the Concorde aeroplane _____

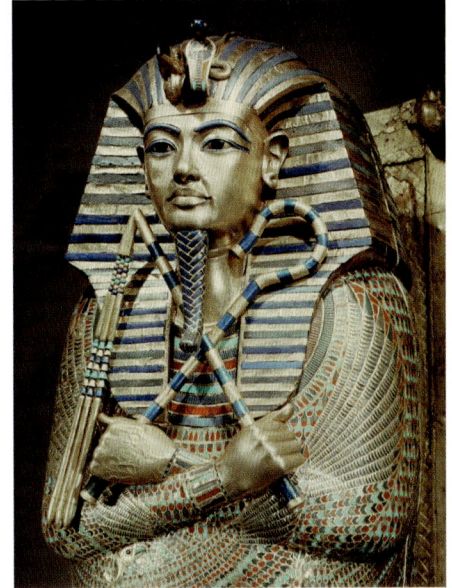

The sarcophagus of Tutankhamun

> ## STUDY SKILL Using the Internet (3)
>
> Many museums have their collections and / or education departments on the Internet. You can study these by logging onto the museum's site, e.g.:
>
> The British Museum — http://www.britishmuseum.org/explore/online_tours.aspx
>
> The Science Museum — http://www.sciencemuseum.org.uk
>
> The Smithsonian Institute — http://si.edu/
>
> Massachusetts Institute of Technology — http://web.mit.edu/museum/
>
> If you are researching a particular object, put it into a search engine with *+museum* e.g. *Guernica+museum*, or ask a question: *Where is Guernica displayed?*
>
> Always credit the site you use, saying when you accessed it, e.g.:
>
> http://www.britishmuseum.org/explore/highlights/highlight_objects/me/m/ottoman_mosque_lamp.aspx (11/03/11)

2 Choose an object from the list. Research it on the Internet and make notes for a two-minute presentation.

- smart phone
- computer
- refrigerator
- washing machine
- internal combustion engine

1 Describe the object.

2 Say why it is significant.

3 Support your ideas with examples, evidence, or reasons (give at least three supporting arguments).

3 Prepare the presentation from your notes. Check the structure of the presentation.

4 Work in small groups. Take turns to give your presentation.

1 The listeners make notes on the objects and supporting arguments in the table.

2 Ask at least one question on each of the presentations.

3 Vote on which object is the most significant.

object	supporting argument 1	supporting argument 2	supporting argument 3
1			
2			
3			
4			
5			

VOCABULARY DEVELOPMENT   Compound adjectives

1 **Read STUDY SKILL** 9.7 Listen and complete the sentences. Read the sentences aloud.

1 The Lewis chessmen are particularly famous for the grumpy-_____ queens.
2 Mirrors were highly-_____ objects.
3 Before the invention of the match, lighting a fire was _____-consuming.

2 9.8 Choose a present or past participle from the box to complete the sentences. Listen and check your answers.

fitting	developed	made	looking	polished

1 Mirrors were made of highly-_____ stone or metal.
2 The tunic of the Hoxne pepper pot was loose-_____ .
3 Some of the chessmen are fierce-_____ soldiers.
4 Only a highly-_____ society could produce such beautiful objects.
5 Before the invention of the sewing machine all clothes were hand_____ .

Compound nouns

3 9.9 Listen to and read the sentences. Mark the main stress on the compound nouns in bold. **Read STUDY SKILL**

1 The **chess set** represents the coming together of three important cultures.
2 A game of chess is essentially a **war game**, a **battlefield**.
3 Perhaps the Lewis chess queens had **toothache**.
4 The object I find significant is the **sewing machine**.
5 These machines meant that **mass production** of clothes was possible.

4 Match a noun in column **A** with a noun in column **B** to form a compound noun.

A	B
1 crime	sites
2 science	department
3 university	fiction
4 plastic	rate
5 web	surgery

5 Put a compound noun from exercise 4 into the questions. Work with a partner. Ask and answer the questions.

1 Do you enjoy reading _____ ?
2 Would you think about having _____ if it were painless and cheap?
3 Is the _____ in your city rising or falling?
4 Which _____ do you visit most often? What do you use them to find out?
5 What _____ do you study in?

tight-fitting

time-consuming

happy-looking

REVIEW

1 🔊 9.10 Listen to a presentation about the match and complete the notes.

Object: THE MATCH
Invented: _____
Significance: changed _____
    SUPPORT & EXAMPLES
1 fire nec. for _____ & _____
2 w/out match   • lighting fires _____ & _____
3 w match cd   • _____

2 🔊 9.10 Listen again. Complete the sentences.

1 A _____ is a simple stick used to light fires.
2 The word _____ means *immediately*.
3 The word _____ means *replaced*.

A match

3 Prepare a short presentation on the significance of the mobile phone, using the notes.

ARGUMENTS	SUPPORT & EXAMPLES
1 can communicate anywhere	1 can phone while travelling – train, bus, car
2 provide security	2 a parents can call children b can make emergency call without money
3 take pictures of events as they happen	3 photos of crimes → arrests of criminals

4 Work with a partner. Take turns to give your presentations.

5 Work with a partner. Ask and answer questions using the compound nouns.

house   credit   note   news   pass   television

1 Which is the most important _____ channel in your country? What sort of programmes does it broadcast?
2 Do you record new vocabulary in a _____book or on the computer? Why?
3 Do you use a _____word to protect your computer? Do you use any other protection on your computer?
4 Which is the most popular _____paper in your country / city? Why do you think it is so popular?
5 Which do you use most often: cash or a _____ card? Why?
6 What _____hold appliance is most important for you? Why?

10 Responsible tourism

LISTENING SKILLS Dealing with longer listenings (1) and (2)
SPEAKING SKILLS Transitions • Dealing with questions
VOCABULARY DEVELOPMENT Dependent prepositions

LISTENING Ecotourism

1 Work with a partner.
Look at Figures 1–3. What do they show?
Discuss, then answer questions a–d.

Figure 1

Figure 2

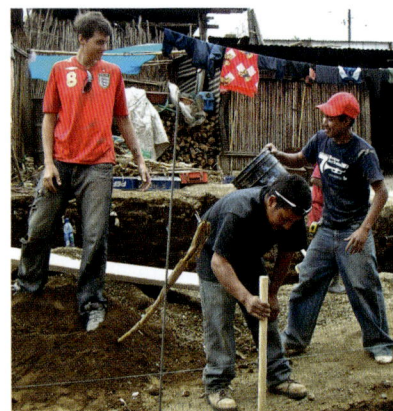
Figure 3

a What are the advantages and disadvantages of tourism?
b How do people choose places for their holidays?
c Which Figure do you think could be an example of ecotourism?
d Can you define what you mean by ecotourism?

2 🔘 10.1 Listen to two radio advertisements for holidays. Which one is for:

a ☐ ecotourism   b ☐ ordinary tourism

3 **Read STUDY SKILL** Look at the mind map about a talk on ecotourism. Add the
words from the box to the diagram.

recycling	energy	local community	environment	reduce pollution
water	plants & animals	tourists	local community	

> ### STUDY SKILL
> ### Dealing with longer listenings (1)
>
> When listening to longer listenings, help
> your understanding by:
> - predicting
> - listening for signposting language
> - taking notes
> - selecting information
> - studying visual aids

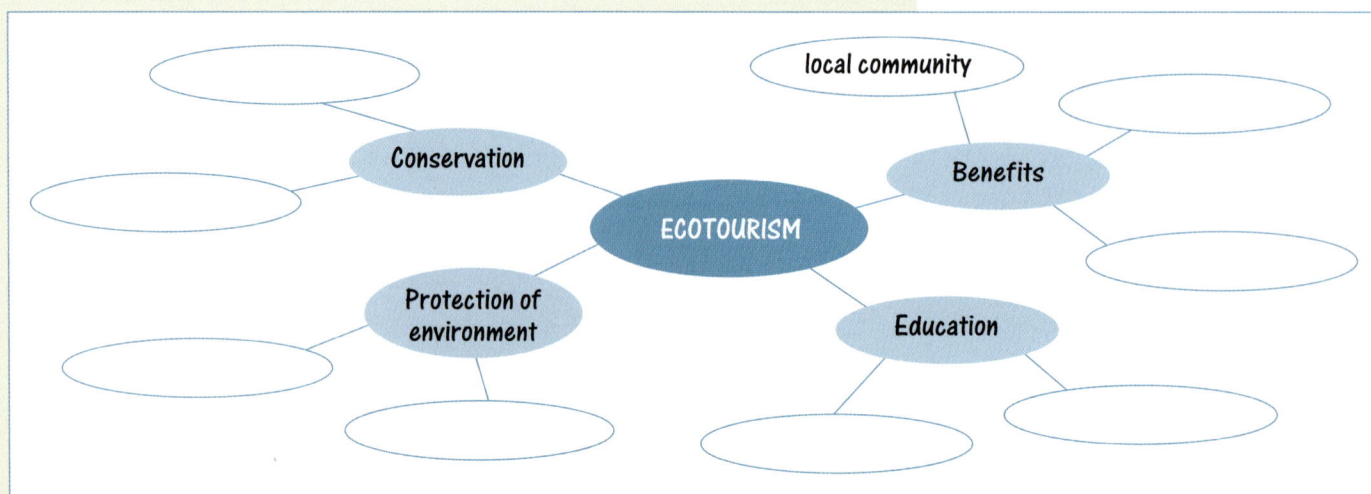

local community

Conservation

ECOTOURISM

Benefits

Protection of
environment

Education

4 You are going to listen to a lecture on ecotourism. Use the question words to write questions about ecotourism.

1 What? _What are the advantages of ecotourism?_
2 Who? _____
3 Where? _____
4 How much? _____

5 🔊 10.2 Listen to the introduction to a lecture on ecotourism. Make suitable headings for notes which you could take during the lecture.

ECOTOURISM

1 _____
2 _____
3 _____
4 _____

6 🔊 10.3 Listen to the lecture and look at Figure 1. Take notes under the headings you made in exercise 5. Did you find the answers to your questions in exercise 4?

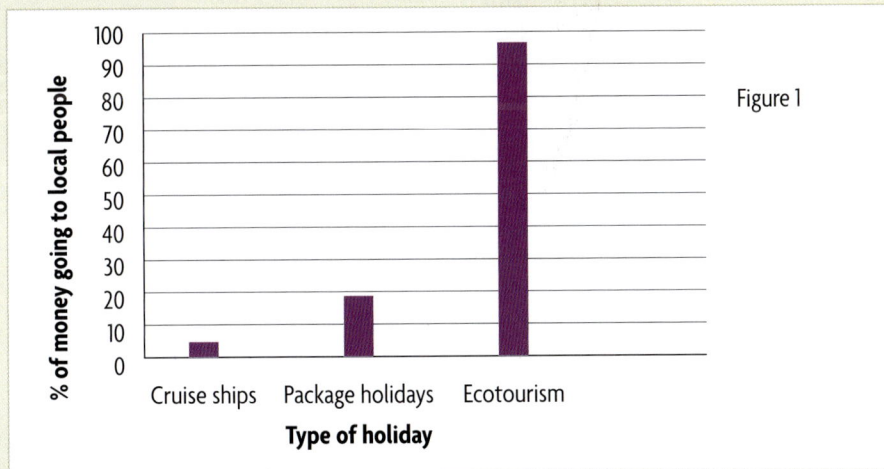

Figure 1

7 Work with a partner. Discuss the questions.

1 Did you have any problems listening to the lecture in exercise 6?
2 What can happen when you are listening to long talks or lectures?
3 What do you do if you have problems?

8 🔊 10.4 Listen to a lecturer giving advice about listening to longer talks. Does she mention the same things as you did in exercise 7?

9 🔊 10.4 Listen again and answer the questions.

1 What happens if you stop concentrating while listening to a talk?

_____

2 What should you do?

_____

3 What three things can you do to help yourself?

_____

10 **Read STUDY SKILL** Work with a partner and discuss your answers to the questions in exercise 9.

SPEAKING Transitions

1 Read STUDY SKILL Put the words in order to complete the sentences.

1 _____ the importance of tourism for the economy.
(section / I'll / this / discuss / in)

2 _____ my first point about the employment of
local people. (to / back / going)

3 _____ the third part of my talk.
(leads / to / me / this)

4 _____ the subject of money brought into the country.
(to / like / turn / I'd / to)

5 _____ the disadvantages of tourism.
(think / about / let's)

2 10.5 Listen and check your answers. Practise saying the sentences aloud.

3 Prepare a two-minute presentation from your notes in
exercise 6 on page 59 on the advantages of ecotourism
over traditional holidays. Work in pairs. Give your
talks. As you are listening to your partner's talk, tick
the transition phrases that are used.

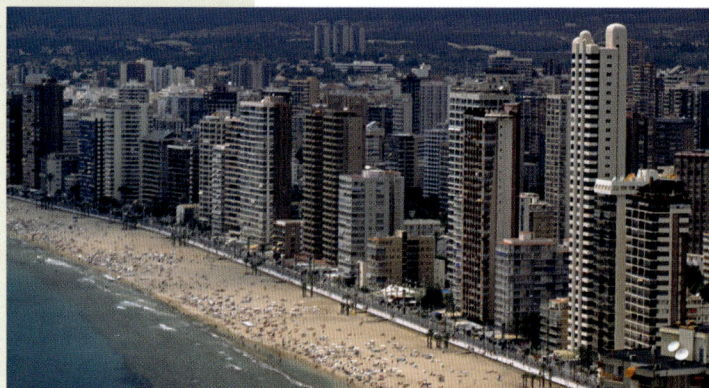
A traditional holiday resort

Dealing with questions

4 Work with a partner. What can you say ...

1 when you don't know the answer to a question?
2 when you want to give yourself some time to answer a question?
3 when you don't understand a question? Read STUDY SKILL

5 Use headings 1–4 to make notes for a two-minute talk on taking a holiday in
your country.

1 Introduction	3 Disadvantages
•	•
•	•
•	•

2 Advantages of a holiday in your country	4 Conclusion
•	•
•	•
	•

6 Work with a partner. Follow the instructions and take turns to give your talk and ask questions, using transition expressions.

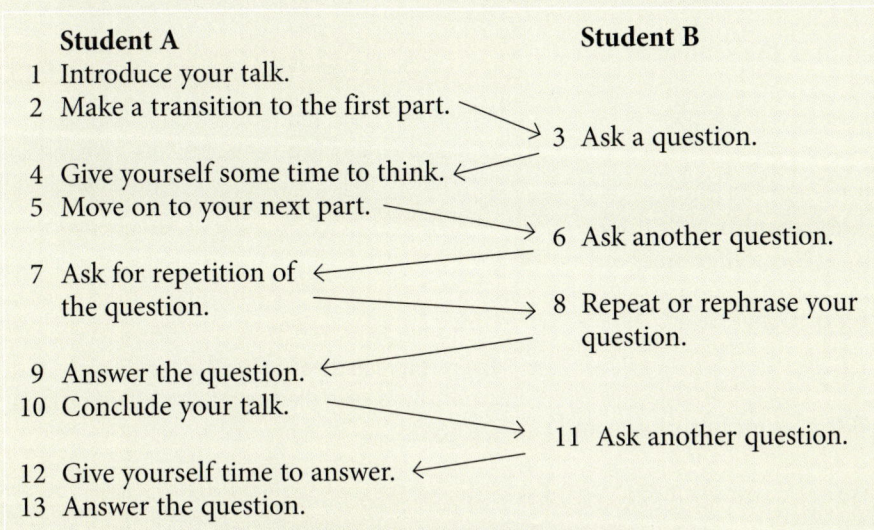

Student A	**Student B**
1 Introduce your talk.	
2 Make a transition to the first part.	
	3 Ask a question.
4 Give yourself some time to think.	
5 Move on to your next part.	
	6 Ask another question.
7 Ask for repetition of the question.	
	8 Repeat or rephrase your question.
9 Answer the question.	
10 Conclude your talk.	
	11 Ask another question.
12 Give yourself time to answer.	
13 Answer the question.	

A presentation

7 Prepare a four-minute presentation on one of the topics or a topic of your choice.

- Communication in the 21st century
- The economic development of my country
- The most important scientific discovery of the last 50 years
- A healthy lifestyle
- An important environmental issue in my country

Think about:

Organization
Research the topic on the Internet
Find some images to illustrate your talk
Make notes
Organize the notes into sections

Language
Use signposting language to:
- introduce the talk
- show transitions
- give examples, explanations, refer to visuals, and so on
- conclude the talk
- ask for and deal with questions

Pronunciation
Check and practise your pronunciation, including:
- word stress
- linking
- pausing between thought groups
- intonation of questions

8 Work in small groups. Take turns to give your talk.

1 Listen and make notes on the main points of each of the presentations.
2 Ask at least one question about each of the presentations.

VOCABULARY DEVELOPMENT
Words and dependent prepositions

1 **Read STUDY SKILL** Circle the correct preposition in the sentences. Use a dictionary to help.

1 The majority of students are interested *for / in / to* doing sport regularly.
2 People who study physics are often good *to / for / at* music.
3 Australian English is quite similar *with / to / about* British English.
4 Who is responsible *to / for / with* organizing the conference?

2 Complete the sentences with the correct preposition. Use a dictionary to help.

1 The police are investigating the cause _____ the fire.
2 What are the differences _____ your new mobile phone and your old one?
3 There was a decrease _____ the use of the multimedia centre last semester.
4 There were over a hundred applications _____ the job.

3 🔊 10.6 Make sentences using the beginnings, a preposition, and an ending. Listen and check your answers.

1 People who suffer	from	cheating in the exam.
2 The student was accused	with	the job of research assistant?
3 How many candidates applied	of	the other students on the best place for a holiday.
4 Aziz did not agree	for	diabetes need to follow a careful diet.

4 Complete the questions with the correct preposition. Work with a partner and take turns to ask and answer the questions.

1 Are you interested _____ economics?
2 At school, which subjects were you good _____ ?
3 What are the main causes _____ air pollution?
4 What are the main differences _____ ecotourism and ordinary tourism?
5 Do you agree _____ the need to restrict the use of cars?
6 Would you ever apply _____ a job abroad?

5 Put the nouns, verbs and adjectives in the box with their prepositions.

spend (money/time)	decrease	good	depend	interested	bad	hopeless
apply concentrate	increase	agree	responsible	disagree	ask	argue

_____ on	_____ at	_____ with	_____ in	_____ for
_____	_____	_____	_____	_____

STUDY SKILL Dependent prepositions

Adjectives, nouns, and verbs are often associated with prepositions. In other words, they have certain prepositions which follow them. For example:

*The student was **disappointed with** his poor exam result.*

*There has been an **increase in** the price of oil.*

*The course **consists of** six different modules.*

The preposition is not stressed in the sentence. It is important to learn the prepositions when you learn the words.

increase in

consist of

good at

agree with

REVIEW

1 You are going to listen to some talks about three tourist destinations. Before you listen, work with a partner and brainstorm what you know about the places. Use the questions in the box to help you.

	Switzerland	Rio de Janeiro	Jordan
Where is it?	Western Europe		
Why do tourists go?			
What is it famous for?	Mountains, chocolate		

Switzerland

2 🔊 10.7 Listen to the talk about Switzerland and answer the questions. How are you going to listen?

1 Why do people go to Switzerland?
2 What problem does the speaker mention?

3 🔊 10.7 Listen again and answer the questions. How are you going to listen?

1 Which country does **not** border Switzerland: Germany, Luxembourg, France, Italy?
2 How do tourists travel to the top of the mountains?
3 Do only advanced skiers go to Switzerland?
4 Name two ways the tourism representatives are solving the problem.

4 🔊 10.8 You are going to listen to part of a tutorial about tourism in Rio de Janeiro. How many people are talking?

5 🔊 10.8 Listen again and answer the questions. Which part would you listen to if you were only interested in:

	1st part	2nd part	3rd part
economics of tourism			
tourist sights			
history of tourism			

6 🔊 10.9 Listen to part of a talk about Jordan. Name three types of tourism there.

1 _____ 2 _____ 3 _____

7 🔊 10.9 Listen again and complete the sentences.

1 Today _____ three main tourist destinations in Jordan.
2 _____ , I will talk about the historical ancient sites.
3 And _____ , I will finish with city tourism.
4 Jordan is famous _____ Petra.
5 There are many other ancient sites _____ Jerash, Madaba and the desert castles.

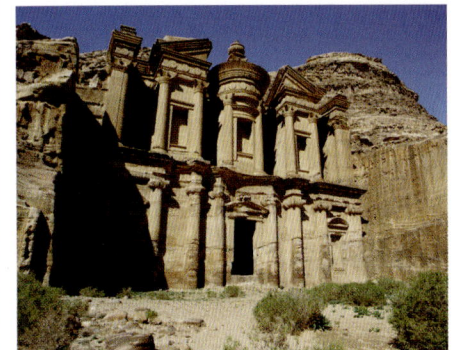
Petra, Jordan

8 Complete the sentences with a preposition, using a dictionary to help you. Discuss the questions in small groups.

1 Are you concerned _____ the environment? What should people do to protect it?
2 Who should take responsibility _____ conserving energy? People or governments?
3 Should flying be more expensive to pay for the pollution it causes? Do people travel _____ plane too often?
4 Would you be interested _____ working in tourism? Why / Why not?

AUDIO SCRIPTS

🎧 1.1

Good morning, everybody. Let me introduce myself: I'm Dr Green and I'm the Senior Tutor for overseas students. So, first of all, I'd like to welcome you to the university. I hope that you will work hard and profit from your time here.

Over the next couple of weeks, I'm going to meet each of you individually, but this morning I just want to give you some general information about the practicalities of life here on the campus: housing, money, and health.

For anything to do with accommodation, please see Mrs Roberts in Room two hundred and fourteen in the Senate Building. That's room two-one-four. For any financial advice, such as setting up a bank account, transferring money, etc, make an appointment to see Dr Reynolds, the Student Financial Adviser, in Room one hundred and seventeen, one-one-seven, in the Admin block. The university health centre is next to Admin and it is a good idea to register with the centre as soon as possible. To do this, you just need to give your personal details to the receptionist. Oh, and you will need to show her your passport and student card.

Right! Any questions so far? No? OK, then let's move on to the reason you're here: your studies. You will be given tutors in your individual subject area, but I'm the person to see if you have any more general concerns about your work. For example, timetable problems or …

🎧 1.2

1 [E= Emily, A= Annie]
   E Hey, Annie, I'm glad I've run into you. Have you got yesterday's book list?
   A Yeah, but not here.
   E Oh! Any chance you could send it to me?
   A Course, what's your email?
   E It's Emily, that's e…m…i…l…y dot shaw, that's s…h…a…w at interfone, i…n…t…e…r…f…o…n…e dot com. All small letters.

2 As you can see from the graph, the urban population has increased rapidly. At the same time, the rural population has fallen dramatically. One explanation for this may be …

3 Please note that Professor Lee's talk on Innovations in Medicine will be held in Room 407, not 507 as stated on the programme.

4 A Excuse me, sorry, excuse me! I'm doing a survey on …
   B Sorry, haven't got the time now.
   A Excuse me, madam. I'm doing a survey on shopping habits and I wondered if I could ask you some questions. It will only take two minutes.
   C Er, well, OK, then.

5 Two people are known to have been killed and ten others injured after an accident involving a main line train and a car which, apparently, had got stuck on a crossing.

🎧 1.3

1 Hello, everyone. My name's Ali El Hendi.
2 Hello, may I introduce myself? I am Dr Phillips.
3 Professor Adwan, isn't it? Hello, I'm Mrs Elliot, Lina Elliot, from Administration.
4 Hi, I saw you in the lecture. I'm Mei…
5 Morning, I'm Elif, Elif Tan, and I'm from Istanbul.

🎧 1.4

Tutor OK, we're all here, so let's get started. As this is the first tutorial of the year, I think it would be a good idea if everyone briefly introduced themselves. I'll start with myself. I'm Dr Peter Black and my particular subject is Accountancy and European Law. And . . .
A Morning everyone. I'm Dilek Sancak and I'm from Izmir, in Turkey. Like you all, I'm studying Accountancy and Finance.
B Hello, my name is Sachit Malhotra from New Delhi, the capital of India. And I'm doing Accountancy and Finance as I'd like to work in an international organization after graduating.
C Hi, I'm Mahmoud Subri and I'm from Jordan. Also, from the capital city, Amman. At the moment I'm more interested in finance and financial institutions, but that may change over the course!

🎧 1.5

1 It's Emily, that's e-m-i-l-y dot shaw, that's s-h-a-w, at interfone, i-n-t-e-r-f-o-n-e, dot com. All small letters.
2 Jim dot grant 32, that's j-i-m, dot g-r-a-n-t 32, at liv, that's l-i-v, dot a.c., dot u.k.
3 G dot reddy, that's r-e-d-d-y, at public underscore info, that's p-u-b-l-i-c, underscore, i-n-f-o, dot gov, that's g-o-v.
4 Buzz dot Peters, that's B-u-z-z dot P-e-t-e-r-s at nsw dot ac dot aus, a-u-s.
5 W-w-w dot researchinfo, that's r-e-s-e-a-r-c-h i-n-f-o dot net, that's n-e-t, forward slash mech hyphen eng, that's m-e-c-h hyphen e-n-g.

🎧 1.6

1 A Give me a ring on my mobile. The number's 076532215.
   B Did you say two two one five?
   A Yeah, two two one five.

2 A Let me make a note of your email address.
   B Sure. It's alan.rodgers13@uwe.ac.uk
   A Was that thirteen or thirty?
   B Thirteen, one three.

3 A Good morning, this is Ella Peters speaking. Is that Chang Li?
   B Yes, it is. Sorry, this is a bad line. I didn't catch your name.
   A Ella, Ella Peters. We met at the conference last week.

4 A It's Paul. Can I pop round and return that book I borrowed? Where's your room?
   B It's Bowland Tower, room nine on the third floor.
   A Third floor?
   B Yeah, …

5 A The best person on this subject is Dr Shehadeh and I advise you to read her latest article.
   B Sorry, could you repeat the name, please?
   A Certainly, Dr Shehadeh, that's S-h-e-h-a-d-e-h.

🎧 1.7

1 detail   2 advise   3 campus   4 mobile   5 thirteen
6 thirty   7 return   8 passport   9 account   10 repeat

🎧 1.8

1 depend   2 tutor   3 accent   4 accept   5 lecture

🎧 1.9

1 sign   2 right   3 what   4 island   5 guest   6 science
7 business   8 column   9 answer

1.10

Lecture 1

Well, good morning and welcome to the Institute of Computing Studies. I'm going to start by giving you an outline of the first five lectures in the History of Computing course. I'd also like to recommend two essential books on your 'Computers: Ancient and Modern' reading list.

Lecture 2

The first and most important question is: what does 'Business Management' mean? Does it mean human resources, that is looking after people at work? Does it mean finance? Does it mean management systems? Well, of course, it means all of these aspects and more!

1.11

Lecture 2

The first and most important question is: what does 'Business Management' mean? Does it mean human resources, that is looking after people at work? Does it mean finance? Does it mean management systems? Well, of course, it means all of these aspects and more!

So, let's get to know each other. I'm Dr Knight and, as well as being Head of Department I will be your tutor for Human Resources. On my right, is Mr Adams who will be teaching you about Finance and Commerce, and this is Dr Williams. She is your Business Systems tutor. Now, today …

2.1

Good afternoon. As I said in the handout, today we'll be looking at what effect being an island, i.e. being separated by water, has on how a country develops economically. I hope you've all read the material I suggested. If you have, you'll know that we'll be using Madagascar and the Philippines as our examples. We'll look in depth at how their industries and agriculture, for example food processing and coffee growing, developed because they are islands.

However, before going into too much detail, let me give you an overview of each island.

As you can see from Map one, Madagascar is situated in the Indian Ocean, off the east coast of Africa. It has a tropical climate around its coast but is dry in the south. Although it is very mountainous, it's also very rich agriculturally. Today its main crops are rice, vanilla, coffee, and sugar cane, and, unsurprisingly, its main industries are food processing and sugar production.

Map 2 shows the second of our two island states, the Philippines. It's very different. It is in fact made up of over 7,000 islands. The Philippines is situated in the Pacific Ocean in South-East Asia. It's got a tropical climate, so two seasons: wet and dry. The main island, Luzon, is mountainous inland. These mountains were once covered in forest. However, increased agriculture, mining, and the wood industry have led to deforestation. The Philippines produce a range of crops including rice, maize, coconuts, and sugar cane. The main industries are mining, petroleum refining, electronics, and food and drink processing.

OK, so that's the brief overview. Now let's turn to how their industries and agriculture were developed as a result of being islands. Just a couple of quick examples to give you the idea. Madagascar's location in the Indian Ocean meant it became an important trading post and so was able to quickly develop the export of its agricultural produce. The Philippines in the Pacific Ocean …

2.2

1 Although it is very mountainous, it's also very rich agriculturally.
2 It has a tropical climate but is dry in the south.
3 However, increased agriculture, mining, and the wood industry have led to deforestation.

2.3

1 Australia is a large country and …
2 Although Australia is a large country, …
3 Most of the population still work in agriculture, which …
4 Most of the population still work in agriculture, but …

2.4

Map 2 shows the second of our two island states, the Philippines. It's very different. It is in fact made up of over 7,000 islands. The Philippines is situated in the Pacific Ocean in South-East Asia. It's got a tropical climate, so two seasons: wet and dry.

2.5

Australia is the largest island in the world. It is situated between the Pacific and Indian Oceans. It has different types of climate because it is so big. It is tropical in the north but has continental weather in the south. The centre is very dry.

2.6

Speaker A I come from Sri Lanka it is a very hot country in south Asia. The climate is tropical. It is famous for its tea production, rice, sugar cane, and rubber. There's lots of flat countryside. There are mountains in the middle it's cooler in the mountains. Our industries are telecommunications, banking, clothing, and tourism.

Speaker B My talk is about Sri Lanka. It is an island located in South Asia, in the Indian Ocean, south of India. The countryside is quite flat in most places. However, there are mountains in the central part of the island. The climate is tropical with two monsoons, that is heavy rains, a year. Although Sri Lanka is particularly famous for its tea production, rice, sugar cane, and rubber are also important agricultural products. The principal industries are telecommunications, banking, clothing, and tourism.

2.7

1 The main produce is coffee.
2 Coffee factories produce a lot of waste.

2.8

	a		b	
1	a	produce	b	produce
2	a	export	b	export
3	a	record	b	record
4	a	present	b	present
5	a	research	b	research

2.9

1 Companies cannot import without an import licence.
2 The group will present its findings tomorrow.
3 The students gave their professor a present when he retired.
4 The secretary made a record of the meeting.
5 If you wish to record this lecture, please do so.
6 Singapore exports a lot of electronic equipment.
7 Two of the main exports from Madagascar are vanilla and coffee.

2.10

In this lecture about island states we're going to turn our attention to Japan and will be looking at three main areas: location and climate, land use and agriculture, and the principal industries.

2.11

In this lecture about island states we're going to turn our attention to Japan and will be looking at three main areas: location and climate, land use and agriculture, and the principal industries.

Firstly, where is Japan? As you can see from the map, it is in north-east Asia and is situated close to Russia and South Korea in the North Pacific Ocean.

The climate is very varied. In the south it is tropical, but in the north it has a cooler, more temperate climate. This allows a range of agricultural products to be grown, for example rice, sugar beet, and fruit. Fishing is also important to Japan's economy. It is estimated that Japanese fishermen catch about 15% of the world's catch.

However, it is the other industries, particularly car manufacturing and the production of electronics goods that are the main sources of Japan's wealth.

2.12

Jamaica is an island in the Caribbean Sea, south of Cuba. It generally has a tropical climate, but the mountainous interior is more temperate. Agriculture is an important part of Jamaica's economy. Sugar cane, bananas, coffee, citrus, yams, and vegetables are all grown on this small island.

2.13

Although Jamaica exports a lot of agricultural products, tourism is its main industry. However, recently the number of tourists has decreased. This has hurt the economy, but the government hopes that tourism will improve again as the global economy grows.

3.1

Well, let's start. Good morning, everyone! My name's Mari Kaplan and I'm here to talk to you about my job. I'm a science journalist, that is, I write scientific news articles. I'd like to tell you what this job involves, the main challenge for a science journalist, what skills you need, and finally, why I chose this profession.

So, what does the job involve? Generally, a science journalist has two main things to do. Firstly, they have to research what's new in the world of science. And secondly, they need to write articles.

First of all, the research: journalists have to find out about new scientific discoveries. How is this done? Well, there are several different ways, for example, by attending academic conferences, and listening to talks; or by visiting research institutes and interviewing the scientists there – finding out about the work they are doing. And a third way we journalists keep informed is by reading academic journals. This is just like any other journalist who needs to know what's happening. But here, the subject is always science!

Next, once they have the news item, the journalist writes an article. This brings me to our main challenge. The key question here is, 'Who's going to read the article?' The kind of article you write depends, of course, on who the reader will be. Let me give you an example. If the article is for a newspaper, most readers will be non-scientists. For this reason, we have to write about scientific subjects in a clear and simple way. This is the challenge!

So, what qualifications and skills does a science journalist need? Well, usually they need a science degree and secondly, they have to be able to write clearly and simply about science subjects, in other words have good communication skills.

I've always been fascinated by science and I've always wanted to communicate my interest to others. That's why I chose this career. I enjoy the challenge of explaining a complex idea in simple terms. I've got the science background because of my degree in Chemistry and the necessary communication skills from a post-graduate degree

in Journalism. So, my education has given me the qualifications and skills for this challenging job.

Now if you have any questions, I'll be happy to answer them.

3.2

A So, Ahmed, what was your first job?

B My first job was with a small TV station. I didn't present the news. I researched the news stories, wrote them, and edited them. Then a presenter read the stories on air.

A Did you want to present the news yourself?

B No, not really. I liked researching and editing. I didn't think about being a presenter because I wasn't very self-confident and you need to be. Anyway, one day someone was ill and they needed a person to announce the programmes, so they asked me. It was just to say a few lines, so I agreed. Afterwards, they told me I have a very good voice and good presentation skills. Apparently, I sound honest and serious and I suppose I look quite good on TV! So that's why the producer suggested more live television work to me. At first I wasn't sure. It's quite stressful speaking live on TV, but eventually I agreed to do it. I started reading the news and I discovered that I really liked it! And so I continued.

A You said you need to be self-confident. What other qualities are important?

B Actually, there are a few other things that are necessary. For instance, sometimes you need to be calm.

A Why's that important?

B Well, many things can go wrong, such as a guest being late. Imagine you're just going to introduce someone onto the programme, and then you hear he or she hasn't arrived. You need to think quickly and find something else to say.

A Are there any other important qualities?

B Yes, you need to stay neutral. Sometimes you have to announce bad news, for example a serious accident or disaster. It's important to keep neutral and not show your feelings.

3.3

1 I didn't think about being a presenter because I wasn't very self-confident.

2 Apparently, I sound honest and serious. That's why the producer suggested more TV work to me.

3 There are a few qualities that are necessary. For instance, sometimes you need to be calm.

4 Well, many things can go wrong, such as a guest being late.

5 Sometimes you have to announce bad news, for example a serious accident or disaster.

6 Most readers will be non-scientists. For this reason, we have to write in a clear and simple way.

7 I've got the science background because of my degree in Chemistry.

3.4

1 He didn't want to become a scientist because …

2 Maya was good at art. That's why …

3 You can find information from different sources, such as …

4 The guest was late because of …

5 Magazines are expensive to produce. For this reason …

6 Newspapers are divided into sections, for example …

7 Photographers specialize in a subject, for instance …

3.5

1　Do you want to be a journalist?
2　What do you want to do?

3.6

1　Do you have any experience?
2　How do you find your information?
3　Is it difficult?
4　What time do you start work?
5　Where is the editor's office?
6　Would you like to work abroad?
7　Why do you want to be a journalist?
8　Have you written the article?

3.7

1　I'm going to write my essay tonight.
2　The café doesn't open till 10.
3　Do you have any free time this afternoon?
4　He doesn't have any experience.
5　I think he'll enjoy the new challenge.
6　When's she starting the job?

3.8

Graphic designers of magazines decide how magazines should look. They choose the colours, the photos, the illustrations and the fonts, and decide the layout of the magazine. That's why they have to be creative and have good visual communication skills. They also need to have good technical skills because they use design software programs such as Adobe® Photoshop. Finally, they should be well organized so they can complete their work in time.

3.9

[I = Interviewer, K = Kalim]
I　So, what are you studying, Kalim?
K　Economics and Business Studies.
I　Is that interesting?
K　Yeah, it's because it's a good combination. The courses are varied but the subjects go well together.
I　And why did you choose it?
K　I really liked Economics at school, that's why I wanted to study it in more detail at university. But I also wanted to do Business Studies. I'm very interested in different aspects of business, such as finance, marketing, and accountancy.
I　And what do you want to do when you've finished?
K　Well, I'm not sure but at the moment, I'd like to work for an international company.
I　I see. Why do you want to do that?
K　Because I think there are lot of possibilities for a good career.

3.10

1　Over a thousand people attended the conference last month.
2　Keiko found a good solution to her transport problem – a bicycle.
3　The radio programme was produced in Sydney.
4　The visiting professor will give a talk on her research.
5　He never wanted to appear on TV.

3.11

[I = Interviewer, V = Vince]
I　So, Vince, what's your job?
V　Well, I'm an online producer, that is, I manage the content of the website of a TV company.
I　OK, so do you write everything that's on the website?

V　No, not everything. Actually, I have four major responsibilities. I choose the articles and then I edit them. Also, I decide on the organization of the site, that's where and how everything appears. And finally, it's my job to make the site attractive to people who visit it.
I　And what skills are important to do this?
V　Well, first of all, good communication skills are essential, for example, it's necessary to be able to write well and communicate with other people. As I said, I decide on the organization of the site, and that's why I need good design skills too. But I don't need to be an IT expert, because the technical creation of the website is done by IT specialists.
I　What makes your job difficult?
V　Well, some sections of the site, such as the news, are updated every two hours. So things are always changing. And there's a problem of space. We have to keep the articles short because of lack of space.
I　And what advice would you give someone who wants to be an online producer?
V　That's simple. Work hard. Work very hard!

3.12

1　Good communication skills are essential, for example, it's necessary to be able to write well.
2　I decide on the organization of the site, and that's why I need good design skills.
3　I don't need to be an IT expert, because the technical creation of the website is done by IT specialists.
4　Some sections of the site, such as the news, are updated every two hours.
5　We have to keep the articles short because of lack of space.

4.1

Today we are going to talk about biomimicry. This is using nature as a model, or how biology can inspire engineering. I will give an example of an invention that was inspired by nature.

The invention I've chosen is one of the most famous examples of biomimicry – Velcro. This is the material that fastens or closes things, such as shoes, clothes, and bags. It's also used to attach objects to materials and keep them in place. The Swiss engineer George de Mestral invented Velcro after observing something similar in nature. One day in the summer of 1948, de Mestral went for a walk in the countryside. When he got home, he noticed some seeds sticking to his coat. Figure 1 shows these seeds on some denim material. De Mestral took the seeds off his coat and examined them closely. He saw that there were very small hooks on the end of them. If you look at the inset in Figure 1 you can see a close-up of one of the seeds and the hooks on it. These hooks attached themselves to anything with a loop, like fibre on clothes, or animal hair. He noticed that the seeds stuck repeatedly, so he could remove the seed and stick it on again many times. He decided to use the same system to make a fabric. After ten years of trying out different things, he produced Velcro.

Velcro is used in clothes, shoes and sandals like those in Figure 2. There are two parts to Velcro. The first part uses hooks and the second, loops, as you can see in Figure 2. The material is usually nylon. When the two parts are pressed together, the hooks catch the loops and hold the fabric in place. When the loops and hooks are separated, they produce a characteristic ripping sound. This is a loud noise, like something tearing. The two parts can be pressed together and pulled apart many times, making Velcro very useful for closing shoes, clothes, and so on.

4.2

Hello, and welcome to today's unit on biomimicry – using nature as a model. I'd like to talk about self-healing plastics. These are plastic materials that can heal or repair themselves. The invention of these materials takes their inspiration from skin.

Look at Figure 3 in the unit. This is a diagram of skin. You can see the surface of the skin at the top, with a few hairs coming through. At the bottom there are red and blue blood vessels. There is also a cut in the surface of the skin. What happens when you cut yourself? Well, your body heals, or repairs itself when special blood cells move from the blood vessels to the cut. These cells stop the bleeding and start the healing, or repairing process.

A material has been developed that acts in the same way. The material is a composite, that is, it's made of different parts. If you look at Figure 4 now, you can see this composite material. One part is fibres. These fibres, which contain resin, go horizontally and vertically through the material and are similar to blood vessels. When a hole forms in the surface of the material, the resin moves to the hole and blocks, or closes it. And so it repairs the hole.

This material can be used to cover the surface of different machines, like aeroplanes, and so improve their safety.

4.3

1 This is the material that fastens or closes things.
2 He noticed that the seeds stuck repeatedly, so he could remove the seed and stick it on again many times.
3 When the loops and hooks are separated, they produce a characteristic ripping sound. This is a loud noise, like something tearing.
4 What happens when you cut yourself? Your body heals, or repairs the cut.

4.4

1 Scientists are studying spider silk. This is the material that spiders make.
2 The silk is made up of polymers. These are long chains of connected molecules.
3 Lizards can walk up walls. How do they manage to adhere to, or stick to the wall?
4 Energy-efficient processes, those that use less energy, are necessary today.
5 Many people talk about sustainable development. This aims to protect the environment for the future.

4.5

It's a really useful object. It's made of plastic and it's small so it's quite light. It has a lot of faces and each one is pentagonal in shape, in other words, it has five sides. In the middle of each face there are three points for putting a plug into. Then there's a cable which is plugged into the wall. It's called an e-ball multi-plug adaptor and it's used to connect plugs from electronic devices to an electrical supply. It's great and everyone should have one!

4.6

My talk today is about how nature has inspired architecture. There are two parts to it – first of all, a description of a natural construction which keeps a constant temperature and, secondly, how architects have copied this system and built a high-rise building with a similar cooling system.

4.7

There are two parts to it / – first of all, / a description of a natural construction / which keeps a constant temperature / and secondly, / how architects have copied this system / and built a high-rise building / with a similar cooling system.

4.8

1 When a hole forms / in the surface of the material, / the resin moves to the hole / and blocks it /or closes it.
2 This material / can be used / to cover the surface of different machines, / like aeroplanes, / and so improve their safety.

4.9

Swimmers and other athletes / are always trying to swim faster,/ using less energy./ To do this,/ they must wear clothes which produce very little friction,/ or resistance,/ when they move through the air / or water./ Scientists who design these clothes / have studied some of the fastest fish in the sea,/ sharks./ They have copied the skins of these animals / and invented a material which reduces friction./ The result / is that swimmers can swim even faster / and be more energy-efficient.

4.10

1 Scientists are inspired by many aspects of nature.
2 The professor thought the exam results were excellent.
3 The students were advised to watch a documentary on television.
4 It is not acceptable to cancel an appointment at the last minute.
5 Schools are concerned about how much exercise children take.
6 The lecture was fairly interesting.

4.11

The design of an office complex and shopping centre in the capital city of Zimbabwe was inspired by nature. The Eastgate Centre in Harare is unusual because it has no air conditioning or heating system, but stays at a constant temperature. The inspiration for its design comes from the African termite. These are small insects that build large mounds, or nests. The temperature inside the mound is kept constant through a system of vents, or openings that the termites open and close. When the vents are open, cooler air from the outside is drawn into the mound while hotter air escapes through chimneys at the top of the mound.

The Eastgate Centre follows the same principles. There are vents at the bottom of the building and chimneys at the top. Cool air is sucked through the building and warm air escapes through the chimneys. In addition, concrete arches protect the building from the sun by shading the windows. As a result, the building uses less than 10% of the energy that other similar buildings use and so the building is an excellent example of an environmentally-friendly design!

5.1

Good morning. Welcome to the international conference on 'Multi-Disciplinary Studies'. I am Dr Felipe Castillo-Fiera, Chair of the Organizing Committee, and I am delighted to see colleagues from all around the world with us today. It is a truly international gathering! I am sure that we are all going to learn a great deal from each other during the next two days, not only from the lectures and seminars, but also from the more informal discussions that take place over coffee and lunch. I am also pleased to see that so many students have joined us, too. Welcome to you all.

Before the first speaker of the day, I would like to point out a few changes in the programme. You will find a copy of the programme in your welcome packs. Everyone found it? Good. So, Dr Maria Smart's talk at 9.30 on 'The role of IT in modern medicine' will be in room 602, not 502. That's room 6-0-2. Dr Smart will be looking at how computer technology is changing nursing and hospital practice.

Professor Anwar's discussion group on Science and the Law in the twenty-first century is now timetabled for 11 o'clock this morning, and not five this afternoon, and will be in Hall B. The discussions will cover both criminal and business law. Because of this change, the university workshop on careers in Engineering and Social Science will now be taking place at 5 o'clock this afternoon in room 46 instead.

Lastly, I'm sure some of you are probably interested in the effects of world trade on global warming, and how to protect the planet. If so, you will be pleased to hear that Professor Carlo Brunetti has kindly agreed to give a talk on this important subject immediately after lunch today, that's at 2.30 in Central Hall.

Well, I think that's all. Let me again welcome you to Madrid and I hope you will all profit from today's events.

5.2

1 How do people see a member of our profession? I think that if you asked a member of the public, they would say an engineer is a man wearing a hard hat and big boots who walks around building sites. But that picture is not true in today's world. There are mechanical or electrical …

2 So, as I was saying, patients' records are now stored electronically. This, of course, means that information can be shared faster and more efficiently between medical staff. It also means that hospitals no longer …

3 To sum up, we've looked at the increasingly important role of studying evidence in laboratories, the use of DNA being the most well known. The police have used this evidence in law courts for many years now. So, let's go on to …

4 No, indeed, Dr Smith, not all the effects of increased international commerce on the environment are negative. As I was saying, studies have shown that some trade can have positive . . .

5.3

[**TO** = Tom O'Farrell, **LP** = Louisa Parker, **RF** = Rebecca Fong, **RW** = Richard West]

TO	Excuse me, may I join you?
LP/ RF	Please do. / Yes, of course.
TO	Thanks, I'm Tom O'Farrell, by the way.
LP	Pleased to meet you. I'm Louisa Parker (**TO** Hello), this is Rebecca Fong, and this is Richard, Richard West.
RF	Hello, there.
TO	Morning.
RW	Pleased to meet you.

5.4

RW	So Tom, what did you think of Dr Smart's lecture?
TO	I thought it was excellent, actually. What about you?
RW	Me, too, in fact it was one of the best presentations I've ever heard!

W1	I agree. Dr Smart is a brilliant speaker.
W2	I'm not sure I agree with 'brilliant', but it certainly was an interesting start to the conference.

5.5

TO	Excuse me, may I join you?
LP/RF	Please do, / Yes, of course.
TO	Thanks, I'm Tom O'Farrell, by the way.
LP	Pleased to meet you. I'm Louisa Parker (**TO** Hello), this is Rebecca Fong, and this is Richard, Richard West.
RF	Hello, there.
TO	Morning.
RW	Pleased to meet you. So Tom, what did you think of Dr Smart's lecture?
TO	I thought it was excellent, actually. What about you?
RW	Me, too, in fact it was one of the best presentations I've ever heard!
LP	I agree. Dr Smart is a brilliant speaker.
RF	I'm not sure I agree with 'brilliant', but it certainly was an interesting start to the conference.

5.6

1 **A** Hello, Alan, what did you think of Dr Smart's talk?
   B Oh, good afternoon. Um, I thought it was very interesting. I particularly liked her description of nursing in the future.
   A I agree. The nursing profession is really going through some interesting changes, isn't it? What about you, Jill? Did you enjoy it?
   C Absolutely, I thought …

2 **C** Good morning.
   D Good morning.
   C Are you enjoying the conference so far?
   D Very much. What about you?
   C Yes, there've been some interesting speakers. What area of multi-disciplinary studies are you involved in?
   D I'm …

3 **E** That was fascinating, wasn't it?
   F Yeah, but I got a bit lost in the middle.
   G Me too, but the handout helped a lot.
   F What handout?
   G Didn't you get the handout? Look, I've …

5.7

1 **A** Hi, Lucy! How's your family?
   B Hello, Sally. They're fine, thanks. And yours?
   A Yes, well, thanks. Are you going …

2 **A** It's a great city for a conference, isn't it?
   B Yes, it is. Is this the first time you've been here?
   A No, actually, I know the city quite well. What about you?
   B This is the first time …

3 **A** I'm from Chicago.
   B Really! Me, too. Where exactly?
   A Hyde Park district, near the university. And you?
   B I'm quite close to you. I've got an apartment …

4 **A** I've finished my essay. How about you?
   B Another five minutes. Will you wait for me?
   A Yeah, sure. I'll just …

5.8

A OK, that's it. I think I'll stop now and have a break. What about you?
B Yes, I think I will too. Are you going for lunch now?
A Yes, I am – what are you going to do?

5.9

A I had an interesting time this weekend.
B Really? What did you do?
A I went on a study trip to Leyburn.
B Leyburn?
A Yeah, it's a small coastal town in the north.
B Oh, and . . .?
A Well, it was fascinating. We did a survey of study habits.
B Study habits?
A Yeah, study habits. It was amazing what we discovered about …

5.10

Really?
And?
Leyburn?
Really?
Really?!

5.11

1 discussion   introduction   conversation
2 biology   archaeology   anthropology
3 medical   musical   physical

5.12

1 administration   2 education   3 pronunciation   4 technology
5 geology   6 zoology   7 electrical   8 mechanical
9 economical

5.13

1 The government is increasing tax on fuel.
2 We are looking into the development of a new multi-disciplinary course in Arabic and American Studies.
3 Thank you for that very interesting talk on the environment.
4 This morning's lecture is on the early history of capitalism.
5 As a teacher, you must not show favouritism in the classroom.
6 I know many of you are interested in a career in journalism.
7 The friendliness of the island people is well known.
8 The accident was caused by the driver's carelessness.
9 Blindness can be caused by bacteria in rivers and lakes.
10 Young children have the ability to learn languages easily.
11 The local community will benefit from the new sports centre at the university.
12 It is important that biological diversity, that is the range of animals and plants, is maintained.

5.14

1 A microorganism is a very tiny living creature.
2 A post-doctorate student is someone who continues to study after they have a Ph.D.
3 An anti-theft alarm is a device in a car that makes a loud noise if someone tries to steal the car.
4 A multinational organization is one that works in many different countries.
5 A biannual event is one that happens twice in one year.

5.15

1 Since the invention of the microchip and the creation of the world-wide web, the way we exchange information has changed dramatically. This series of lectures will investigate how the nature and content of communication has changed. Hence, the title: *From speech to social networking*.
2 This field of study can be divided into several important areas. For example, we'll be looking at the importance of the role of the HR department, that's human resources, in a modern company as well as the basic principles behind the production of goods and services.

3 When you tell people what you are studying, they will usually think that you design houses, theatres, and other buildings. However, as you are aware, our profession involves far more than that. For example, many of our graduates go on to work in urban planning departments in cities across the country or work …

5.16

1 A What do you think, Mia?
  B I'm not so sure but …
  C Surely it's quite clear that …
  A Please let Mia finish.
  C Sorry, Mia.
  B As I was saying, it's …

2 A I absolutely agree with Dr Smith's point.
  B Well, I'm afraid that my research team produced very different results. How would you explain that, Dr Smith?
  C Obviously I would have to study your results more thoroughly in order to …

3 A How's the course going?
  B Not bad actually. But there's an awful lot of work!
  C Yeah, for my course, too. But most of it's research and reading, which I really like.
  D Lucky you! I have to write two or three essays a week!

5.17

1 A Beautiful day, isn't it?
  B Glorious. I'm pleased to be here – it's rainy and cold at home!
  A Ah, and where's 'home'?

2 A What do you think of the election results?
  B I'm pleased. I was really hoping they'd win. What about you?
  A I'm not so sure. I really thought it would be a victory for …

5.18

A Is this your first term?
B Yes, it is. What about you?
A Yes! And I'm having problems finding my lecture room!
B What lecture is that?
A Archaeology 101.
B Really?
A Yes. Why?
B I'm studying archaeology, too!

6.1

1 This was an enormous improvement. In fact, this functional food has probably saved many young lives and prevented millions of people from having low intelligence, just by simply and cheaply adding iodine to salt.
2 Now let's turn to another example of good functional foods. These are ones containing the fatty acids Omega 3s, which scientists believe reduce the risk of heart disease. There is real evidence now that they may also have beneficial effects on other diseases, such as some cancers, and …
3 Indeed there is some evidence that probiotics may attack certain infections. However, there is a need for more research and information about their safety and use before we can be sure.

6.2

This is very important.
It's a wonderful invention.
I'm sure.
This has been clearly shown.
There is some truth in that, but …
Maybe.

6.3

Part 1

Good morning. Today's lecture is about 'functional foods'. What are they and what do they claim to do?

First of all, what are functional foods? Well, the name 'functional foods' was invented in Japan about 30 years ago in the mid-80s. Clearly, all food is functional, as it provides nutrition, taste, and so on. But 'functional foods' are foods which give extra benefits such as improving health and reducing the risk of disease. These functional foods are made by adding minerals, vitamins, or live bacteria to ordinary food.

First, let's look at an example of a type of food that contains extra minerals. We all know that minerals are very important for health. Take the example of iodine. If a child doesn't get enough of it, then their brain doesn't develop normally. But iodine is also essential for adults. Not having enough can cause serious problems in people of all ages. This is a problem that affects two billion people, that's around 30% of the world's population. So, a functional food was produced to try and solve this problem, by adding iodine to salt. The results have been amazing. Let's look at Tanzania. In the early 1990s, 42% of the population in Tanzania were lacking iodine, that's more than four out of ten people. Iodine was then introduced into salt and the results were very promising. Just twelve years later 94% of children had normal iodine levels in their bodies. This was an enormous improvement. In fact, this functional food has probably saved many young lives and prevented millions of people from having low intelligence, just by simply and cheaply adding iodine to salt.

6.4

Now let's turn to another example of good functional foods. These are ones containing the fatty acids Omega 3s, which scientists believe reduce the risk of heart disease. There is real evidence now that they may also have beneficial effects on other diseases, such as some cancers, and it is possible that Omega 3s improve brain function in older people.

They can't be made by the body and so must be eaten. They're found naturally in certain foods like some fish. However, now food manufacturers add Omega 3s to common foods, such as fruit juice, eggs, and milk. Eating these foods with added Omega 3s can have real health benefits.

A third example of functional foods are ones with probiotics in them. These are live microorganisms, or good bacteria, which have a health benefit. Probiotics are added to foods like yogurts and yogurt drinks. Scientists think that they help the body fight diseases. Indeed there is some evidence that probiotics may attack certain infections. However, there is a need for more research and information about their safety and use before we can be sure.

6.5

1 Taking vitamin pills might not always be good for you.
2 A poor diet possibly causes brain damage.
3 Some people believe that eating fish is good for the brain.
4 Yogurts that contain live bacteria may be better for you.
5 Experts claim that superfoods such as blueberries help prevent cancer.
6 A little chocolate every day is probably not bad for you.
7 Too much fat in your food can cause heart disease.
8 Doctors think that not enough physical exercise is bad for your heart.
9 It is possible that a stressful lifestyle is a cause of cancer.

6.6

1 Almost 400 people attended the lecture.
2 Over 400 people attended the lecture.
3 The equipment cost nearly €500.
4 The equipment cost more than €500.
5 The lecture lasted for over an hour.
6 The lecture lasted for less than an hour.

6.7

A Today I'm going to talk about a way of making food safer. We know that we can only keep fresh food, such as meat or fruit, for a short time because it goes bad. This is because bacteria attack the food and start to break it down. Keeping the food cold in the fridge stops the bacteria from growing quickly. Cooking or heating the food to a high temperature also stops the bacteria from growing. Another way is to kill the bacteria on the food, without changing the food itself. This can be done by adding special viruses or 'bacteria eaters' called *bacteriophages*.

B Could you repeat that name, please?

A Yes. Bacteriophages. These viruses were discovered in 1915, almost a hundred years ago. They have two advantages. Firstly, they don't attack humans or animals, so they don't cause any diseases. And secondly, they only attack specific bacteria. They don't kill good bacteria, such as those found in probiotics. Do you know what I mean by probiotics?

C Yes, they are bacteria that are added to food to give a health benefit.

A Exactly. Now these bacteriophages can be added to food to kill some of the bad bacteria.

B Could you explain how they are added to the food?

A Yes, a liquid solution of the bacteriophages is sprayed onto the surface of the meat, or other food. Do you have any other questions?

C Are these bacteriophages completely safe?

A Studies so far have shown that they are, although some scientists believe that more testing needs to be done.

C So what you're saying is that there may be some danger from using bacteriophages on food…

6.8

1 Do you eat fresh fruit every day? What do you eat?
2 What do you do to manage a stressful lifestyle?
3 Do you think regular physical exercise is important? What exercise do you take?
4 Do you believe functional foods have beneficial effects on health? Give some examples.
5 Do you think a small amount of chocolate is good for you? Why / Why not?
6 Can certain foods help you develop high intelligence? Give some examples.

🔊 6.9

[**I** = Interviewer, **DR** = Dr Reinhardt]

I It is common today to add vitamins and minerals to foods and sell them as functional foods that are healthier than other foods. But do these functional or fortified foods really have beneficial effects on our health? Today I'm talking to Dr Reinhardt, head of the Food Science and Technology department at the university. Dr Reinhardt, are these foods really better for us than ordinary foods?

DR First of all, it depends what you mean by ordinary foods. If we are talking about processed food, which has lost a lot of its nutrients, or a lot of the fast food that people eat today, yes, functional foods are probably much better. This is because functional foods have extra minerals or vitamins. These are added because they are lost from the foods during processing; or sometimes these ingredients just don't occur naturally in the foods.

I So, do we need to eat them?

DR Yes, people who have a poor diet, who eat the same types of food every day, can suffer from a lack of essential vitamins or minerals. And the reasons for a poor diet can be varied. Some people living in poorer countries do not have any choice. They eat what they can. Other people just eat badly, even though they could have a balanced diet. In both these cases, eating functional foods can be beneficial. But for those of us who eat well, and by that I mean a well-balanced diet with plenty of fruit and vegetables, enough protein, and not too much fat or carbohydrates, functional foods are probably unnecessary.

I And is there a big market for functional foods?

DR Yes, this is a growing business. It's been estimated that the market grew 9.6% in this country last year. That's nearly 10% in one year! The business is worth just under one and a half billion euros today. And all the time new products are being developed and sold in our shops. In fact, in just over two years, the number of foods with added Omega 3s has increased by over 68%! And that's just one example! …

🔊 6.10

I So Dr Reinhardt, what is the future of functional foods?

DR The market will probably continue to grow and I think more substances like Omega 3s will be developed. Nowadays people are concerned about their health and the food they eat and this isn't going to change. There's always going to be an interest in new foods and food companies are researching into them all the time. They are developing ones that may protect people from diseases and foods that could even increase intelligence. The future of functional foods is certainly very exciting and I believe we'll see some great new products in our supermarkets.

🔊 7.1

[**P** = Presenter, **ER** =Emma Reynolds]

P Good evening and welcome to the last in our present series of *Heroes*. As regular listeners will know, each week we invite one guest to present their hero to us, and another guest to discuss that choice.
This week we have the well-known author and Professor of Tropical Diseases, Dr Emma Reynolds, and her hero is Dr Elizabeth Garrett Anderson, who was born in London in 1836. So, Emma, why choose Garrett Anderson as your hero, or should I say heroine?

ER Well, for many reasons, actually. First of all, …

🔊 7.2

P Good evening and welcome to the last in our present series of *Heroes*. As regular listeners will know, each week we invite one guest to present their hero to us, and another guest to discuss that choice. This week we have the well-known author and Professor of Tropical Diseases, Dr Emma Reynolds, and her hero is Dr Elizabeth Garrett Anderson, who was born in London in 1836. So, Emma, why choose Garrett Anderson as your hero, or should I say heroine?

ER Well, for many reasons, actually. First of all, in 1865, at the age of 29, she became the first woman in England to become a doctor, and so gave other women all over the country the opportunity to also practise medicine.

P And that's why she's your heroine?

ER To my mind, it's not just her great achievement. It's the way she did it. She was a strong and determined character and nothing stopped her.

P What do you mean?

ER Let me tell you a bit about her childhood. She was born in 1836 in East London, which was a very poor part of the city, and she was one of 12 children. But she went to a good school and decided she wanted to be a doctor. But at that time, it was impossible for women to study medicine. Instead of giving up, she enrolled as a nursing student and slipped into classes for doctors.

P Didn't anybody notice?

ER Well, of course they did and banned her from the classes.

P So, what did she do next?

ER She enrolled in the Society of Apothecaries, or what we'd call chemists, or pharmacists, today, passed the exams and in 1865 received a certificate to practise medicine.

P So, that was the end of the fight?

ER Not exactly. And this is why I admire her so much. Although she could practise medicine, she was still determined to get a proper medical degree.

P But, I thought you said that was impossible.

ER It was in England. But that didn't stop her. She taught herself French and then took a medical degree at the University of Paris. In my opinion, this was a huge achievement.

P Definitely a role model for determination and hard work!

ER Indeed! But she went further. She founded a hospital in London for women, staffed completely by women. This was a first in England. And, by the way, the hospital still exists!

P So, how would you sum up your decision to make Elizabeth Garrett Anderson your heroine?

ER For me, it's her character: determined, hard-working, courageous, and generous, especially to other women who wanted to follow her into medicine. And, of course, her achievements: becoming the first woman doctor, founding a hospital for women, and becoming an example for other women. A great life!

P Thank you Emma. Now, I'd like to bring in Dr Adam Robbins. Dr Robbins is …

7.3

[J = James, Y = Yasmin, P = Parvin]

J I don't think that Garrett Anderson is a great hero. To my mind, a hero should be someone who's found a cure for a disease, for example someone like Alexander Fleming, the Scottish biologist who discovered penicillin. Apparently, he saw many soldiers die from blood poisoning in the First World War and wanted to find something that would stop this happening. And he did! I mean, penicillin has saved millions of lives. What do you think, Yasmin?

Y I believe that choosing a hero is a very personal thing. I mean, for me, my grandfather's a hero. But, with regard to Fleming, I think he was one of the great 20th century scientists, but not the greatest. Personally, I'd vote for Crick and Watson. Crick was an English physicist as well as a biologist while the American, Watson, was a biologist and zoologist. Working together, their discovery of DNA has changed the world of medicine.

P Absolutely, but what about someone like Florence Nightingale? In my opinion, she's a real English hero. You know, she was the founder of modern nursing. She started simple things like, well, just by getting doctors and nurses to wash their hands between patients, she saved thousands and thousands of lives. I mean, that's amazing, isn't it? And, what's more, she was also a great statistician and she …

7.4

I would like to tell you about my hero, the inventor Carl von Linde. Firstly, I'll tell you about his background, then I shall talk about his achievements, and, finally, tell you why I think he is a hero.

So, first of all some background. Von Linde, who was born in Berndorf in Germany in 1842, was originally expected to study religion like his father. However, he decided he wanted to be an engineer so he went to Zurich to study and then worked as an engineer before becoming a university professor.

Now, I'll tell you about his main achievement. Von Linde invented something that we could not live without today: the refrigerator or 'fridge'. People had used ice boxes for many years to try to keep food fresh and to stop it rotting and going bad. With the invention of the fridge, this became possible to do properly for the first time.

In my opinion, von Linde is a hero for two main reasons. Firstly, I admire him for his character. Although he was expected to study religion like his father, he knew he wanted to be an engineer. That must have been very difficult for him and his family. Secondly, I think that the fridge is one of the most useful inventions of all time. It is impossible for many of us now to imagine what life was like before it. Fridges are relatively cheap and reliable and available for everyone.

To sum up, for me von Linde is a hero because he succeeded in producing something everyone uses.

7.5

1 She was born in East London, which was a very poor part of the city.
2 Madame Curie, who was Polish, lived most of her life in France.
3 Lancaster University, where I studied, was founded in 1964.

7.6

A Well, I believe, a real hero is an ordinary person who does something extraordinary. You know, like that group of blind climbers who conquered Everest. Now, they're heroes in my opinion.

B I disagree because that's a personal act of heroism. By 'hero' I mean someone who is respected and admired for doing something that has an effect on the lives of many people.

C I agree. A hero has to be someone who has had a real impact on how we live.

A Yes, I suppose you're right. In that case, I think I'll vote for Alexander Fleming. His discovery of penicillin has saved millions of lives.

B Yes, that's not a bad suggestion, but what about …

7.7

1 I'm terribly sorry, but I don't think you're right.
2 I think you could be mistaken.
3 I think you could be wrong.
4 I think you're wrong.
5 No, you're wrong.

7.8

Lee and I argued initially about our choice of hero. I had chosen Marie Curie but Lee had suggested Jonas Salk. We discussed it for some time and then decided to study the effects of both people's work more deeply. Then I discovered how Jonas Salk had developed the vaccine for polio and that this vaccine, and a later one, eradicated polio around the world and saved millions of lives. So, finally I also chose Salk.

7.9

A So, Lee. It's your turn for a presentation. Who have you chosen?

B My choice of hero is Jonas Salk, the American virologist. First of all, I'll give you some background information. Then, I'll tell you about his career and achievements, and finally, I'll explain why I think he is a hero.

7.10

So, Jonas Salk was born in New York City in 1914. Although his parents were immigrants and had little formal education, they wanted their children to be well educated. As a result, Jonas was the first member of his family to go to college. At first he studied law but then changed to medicine. It was during his medical training that he developed an interest in viruses.

After medical school he worked with the microbiologist Thomas Francis Jr. to try and discover a vaccine for influenza, or 'flu' as it is more commonly known. This research was successful, and an anti-flu vaccine was developed. Salk's interest then turned to the disease poliomyelitis, or 'polio'. In 1947 he became Head of the Virus Research Laboratory at the University of Pittsburgh and started working on a polio vaccine. In 1952 he tested the first vaccine on volunteers including himself and his family. In 1955, after further testing, the discovery of a polio vaccine was made public, and Salk become a national hero. This vaccine, and its development later by Albert Sabin, has saved lives all over the world.

There are two main reasons why I chose Jonas Salk. Firstly, because his work on both flu and polio vaccines has saved millions of lives. Not only that, but today polio has been almost completely eradicated from the world. My second reason is that Salk refused to patent his discovery and make a profit from it as he wanted the vaccine to be as cheap and freely available as possible. So, it is the combination of Salk's medical genius and his generosity that, in my opinion, makes him a hero.

7.11

A Thank you, Lee. That was very interesting. Now, some reactions. Suheir, what do you think?

B Well, it's true that Salk discovered the first polio vaccine, but it was Sabin's vaccine that was more generally used and saved more lives. So, I think that Sabin's more of a hero than Salk.

A Interesting. Peter?

C Well, I know what Suheir means. But it was Salk that did the first vital studies. Without this work, Sabin could not have produced his vaccine. So, in my opinion, Salk is a great man.

◎ 7.12

Albert Sabin, who was born in 1906, discovered the first oral polio vaccine. It was much easier to vaccinate people, especially children, by giving the vaccine on a sugar lump than injecting them with a needle. Using this vaccine, which is so easy to give, polio has been practically eradicated and millions of lives have been saved.

◎ 8.1

1 **A** Excuse me! Would you mind answering a few questions?
  B What about?
  A We're doing a survey about how people communicate. Email, blogs, phone calls, texts, and so on. It'll only take a few minutes.
  B OK then.
  A Which way of communicating do you use the most – texting, email, phoning, or social networking like Facebook?
  B Yes, I use Facebook. But, I suppose, texting the most. Yes, I text a lot. I think it's really useful.
  A And do you use the phone?
  B Sure. But it's cheaper to text.
  A And Twitter? Do you use Twitter?
  B Don't use it, no. Never.
  A What about emails?
  B Yes, every day.
  A And can I ask your age range? 18–24, 25–30?
  B 18–24.
  A Thank you very much for your help.

2 **A** Excuse me! Can I ask you a few questions about ways you communicate?
  B Yes, as long as it doesn't take too long.
  A Do you use an online social networking site?
  B A what, sorry?
  A A networking site, like Facebook or MySpace?
  B Never.
  A Could you tell me why?
  B I think it's a waste … Don't know why people use them. They're completely useless.
  A And do you send texts or speak on the phone?
  B Well, it depends. If it's urgent, or to a close friend, I'll call. But if it can wait, then a text.
  A And emails?
  B Use them all the time. They're essential.
  A Thanks, and could you tell me your age range?
  B Between 45 and 50.

3 **A** Good morning, I'm doing a survey on communicating. Could I ask you a few questions?
  B Yeah, of course.
  A Do you use an online social networking site, like Facebook or MySpace?
  B Yes, I do.
  A And why, may I ask?
  B Well, I like my friends … I like to tell them what I'm doing.
  A Do you use Twitter?
  B Hmm, yes I do.
  A And do you have a blog?
  B Yes.
  A Er, how often do you update it?
  B Every day. No, not that much. Four times a week, say.
  A And finally, could you give me your age?
  B Yeah, I'm 26.

◎ 8.2

1 **A** Hello there! We're doing a survey on mobile phones. Could you answer a few questions, please?
  B Yes, sure.
  A Do you have a mobile phone?
  B Yeah, I do.
  A And what do you mainly use your mobile phone for?
  B Phoning and sending and receiving texts.
  A And um, how many calls do you make a day?
  B Well, it depends. Between 5 and 10.
  A Er, how many texts do you send and receive a day?
  B Probably about 15.
  A Do you use Internet access on your phone?
  B No, no … never.
  A What other applications do you use on your phone?
  B Let me think. Yeah, I use the calendar a lot.
  A Thank you very much for your time.

2 **A** Excuse me! May I ask you a few questions, please?
  B Yes, OK.
  A Do you have a mobile phone?
  B Yeah, of course.
  A And what do you mainly use it for?
  B Oh, sending texts.
  A And phone calls?
  B Yes, of course, but I send more texts.
  A And do you use Internet access on your phone?
  B Yes, sometimes – to check my emails.
  A What other applications do you use?
  B Um, the camera.
  A And games? The calendar? Listening to the radio?
  B No, never.
  A Well, thank you very much for your help.

3 **A** Excuse me! Would you mind answering a few questions?
  B No, not at all.
  A Do you have a mobile phone?
  B Oh yes!
  A What do you mainly use it for?
  B Everything. Phone calls, texts, emails, Internet … I couldn't live without it.
  A What is the most important function for you?
  B Phone calls, I suppose. It is first after all, a phone.
  A Do you have other applications?
  B Sure, I've got lots of apps.
  A What kind of apps?
  B Every kind. GPS, train times, weather, games, dictionary, translator. To be honest, I can't even remember what some of them are for. I've probably got over fifty by now.
  A And do you …

◎ 8.3

1 We're doing a survey.
2 Do you have a mobile phone?
3 I couldn't live without it.
4 I've got lots of apps.
5 What kind of apps?
6 I can't even remember.

8.4

A Excuse me! I'm doing a survey on the Internet. May I ask you a few questions, please?

B OK.

A Do you have the Internet at home?

B Yes, I do.

A What kind of connection do you have? Dial-up? Broadband?

B Er, broadband.

A Is it a wireless network?

B Yes, it is. I can use the Internet all over the house.

A Is the speed of the Internet connection: a) very fast, b) fast, c) slow or d) very slow?

B Sorry, could you repeat the options, please?

A Of course. Is the speed of the Internet connection: a) very fast, b) fast, c) slow or d) very slow?

B I'd say a) very fast.

A What do you do if there's a problem with the connection?

B I phone the helpline.

A Is the helpline service: a) excellent, b) very good, c) good, d) poor, or e) very poor?

B Very good, though it is a bit slow sometimes.

A Thank you and …

8.5

1 Excuse me! Would you mind answering a few questions?
2 Good afternoon! May I ask you a few questions?
3 Excuse me! Could you answer some questions for me?
4 Thank you for your time.
5 Thank you very much for answering my questions.

8.6

The survey was carried out to find out about Internet connections at home. A small group of twenty-five people, between the ages of 18 and 24 were questioned in the street. People were asked about the type of connection they had and their satisfaction with the service.

As we expected of this age group, 100% of the people questioned had Internet access at home. The majority of people, almost 80%, had broadband, and described the speed as 'very fast' or 'fast'. Most of these people had a wireless network. The remaining 20%, who had dial-up connection, found it slow or very slow. When there was a problem, the helpline service used was found to be good or very good, for most people, although a few described it as 'poor'.

To conclude, this short survey shows that most of the young people questioned have broadband connection at home and are generally satisfied with the service.

8.7

1 I was absolutely exhausted.
2 The report was absolutely fascinating.
3 Kalim found the exam absolutely impossible.
4 The winters were absolutely freezing.
5 The arrangements for the conference were absolutely perfect.
6 The lecture theatre was absolutely enormous.
7 Lina was absolutely terrified before doing her presentation.

8.8

1 **A** So, have you got any ideas for our presentation? What do you think we should talk about?

B Well, I thought we could do something on using mobile phones.

C Hmm. Not very original. What about access to the Internet?

A What do you mean?

C I mean, where and how people access the Internet. At home, university, in parks.

B Parks?

C Yes, in some cities, there's free Internet in the parks.

A Yeah, and in some cafés too. I suppose we could do that. And who pays? At home you have to pay for Internet access, at university it's free, and so on.

B Yes, OK then. Let's do that. Access to the Internet. We can do some research on the net.

2 **A** How's it going?

B What?

A How are you getting on?

B Fine. I've found lots of stuff about free access in different countries and in different places and …

C Good. Now, we need to talk about visuals.

A Visuals?

C Yes, are we going to make a Powerpoint presentation? Or give out some photocopies. Or maybe we could make a big poster.

A Yeah, I think we should use a Powerpoint.

B Yeah, but not too many … and I mean there shouldn't be too much information on each slide.

C No, of course not. If you give me the information that you've found, I can make some Powerpoint slides of it.

B OK that would be great.

A Yes, I'll mail you mine.

3 **A** Thanks for the Powerpoint slides. They look really good. I think it's all ready now.

B Yeah, they're great. But I'd really like to practise the talk, all together.

C That's a good idea. But when and where?

A What about straight after the class on Tuesday?

B No, I've got a tutorial then. What about after lunch, Tuesday?

C Yes, but before 5, as I've got football practice then.

B OK. Does two o'clock suit everyone?

A Yeah, fine.

C OK. And where?

B Well, let's meet at the main entrance to the library and I'll book one of those small workrooms.

8.9

1 **A** So, have you got any ideas for our presentation? What do you think we should talk about?

B Well, I thought we could do something on using mobile phones.

C Hmm. Not very original. What about access to the Internet?

A What do you mean?

C I mean, where and how people access the Internet. At home, university, in parks.

B Parks?

C Yes, in some cities, there's free Internet in the parks.

A Yeah, and in some cafés too. I suppose we could do that. And who pays? At home you have to pay for Internet access, at university it's free, and so on.

B Yes, OK then. Let's do that. Access to the Internet. We can do some research on the net.

8.10

2 **A** How's it going?
   B What?
   A How are you getting on?
   B Fine. I've found lots of stuff about free access in different countries and in different places and …
   C Good. Now, we need to talk about visuals.
   A Visuals?
   C Yes, are we going to make a Powerpoint presentation? Or give out some photocopies. Or maybe we could make a big poster.
   A Yeah, I think we should use a Powerpoint.
   B Yeah, but not too many … and I mean there shouldn't be too much information on each slide.
   C No, of course not. If you give me the information that you've found, I can make some Powerpoint slides of it.
   B OK that would be great.
   A Yes, I'll mail you mine.

9.1

This week, I shall talk about the game of chess and the Lewis chessmen, and give three reasons for their significance. The chess set I have in mind was found on the Isle of Lewis, off the north-west coast of Scotland in 1831. It was originally made in the twelfth century, probably in Norway. There are three reasons why I think these chessmen are significant.

Firstly, they represent a tradition of playing games that human beings have enjoyed from the beginning of time, and in this way connect us to people who have lived before us, in the past, showing us what links humanity through time and place.

Secondly, this chess set represents the coming together of three important cultures and traditions: India where the game originated in the 6th century; the Islamic world which brought the game to Europe; and Mediaeval Christian Europe, which adopted the game enthusiastically.

Lastly, the game of chess is essentially a war game, a battlefield, though fortunately one where no one is hurt. It shows how human beings can transform war into something more positive; perhaps football would be another example of this.

9.2

I would like to suggest that the mirror is a significant object. Mirrors were first made of polished metal or obsidian, a type of stone, around 6000 BCE. The earliest example was found in Çatal Hüyük in present-day Turkey. The Romans were responsible for creating the first mirrors made of glass. So, why is the mirror a significant object? Well, for the first time, human beings could actually see themselves. This may seem very obvious today, but imagine what it was like for someone to see their own image for the very first time. They could look at their own faces, and could even improve their appearance with cosmetics if they wished. Furthermore, the mirror changed the way people 'saw' the world in two important ways. Firstly, with a mirror, the image is reversed; that is, right becomes left, and secondly, with a mirror you can see behind you. This must have seemed almost magical to our ancestors.

9.3

1 The chessmen were carved, that is cut, from the teeth of whales and one set was painted red.
2 The first glass mirrors were made by the Romans. The method of making these mirrors convex, which means curved out, changed little until the 15th century.
3 Mirrors were highly prized and were often put into the graves, in other words the places where people were buried, of dead soldiers and leaders so that they could take them to the next world.

9.4

This silver pepper pot is in the shape of the bust, or top half, of a woman with holes in the bottom to release the pepper. The woman herself is wearing a loose tunic, or dress, and she wears gems, valuable stones, set in a gold necklace around her neck. Her hair is beautifully prepared. She would probably have had a hairdresser to do it for her. She is clearly a wealthy woman, as only a person with money could afford to have pepper with their meals.

9.5

This week's item is the Hoxne pepper pot. It was just one object among thousands found in a field in November 1992. It is significant for two reasons: firstly, it shows us how important and how far-reaching trade was in the 4th century CE. The pot was found in England, but pepper only grew in India. So, we know that pepper was shipped first to Egypt, and then transported around Europe and North Africa. The pot is also significant because it tells us a lot about society in the Roman Empire in the late 4th century.

This silver pepper pot is in the shape of the bust, or top half, of a woman with holes in the bottom to release the pepper. The woman herself is wearing a loose tunic, or dress, and she wears gems, valuable stones, set in a gold necklace around her neck. Her hair is beautifully prepared. She would probably have had a hairdresser to do it for her. She is clearly a wealthy woman, as only a woman with money could afford to have pepper with their meals.

Archaeologists believe that the treasure, including the pepper pot, was hidden around the end of the 4th / beginning of the 5th centuries. This was probably because the Roman Empire was beginning to break up and there was less security so rich people wanted to hide their money and jewels.

As well as the pepper pot, over 15,000 coins were found and more than 200 other gold and silver items.

Of the coins, just under 570 were solid gold and just over 14,000 were silver. There were also about 100 silver spoons and three other pepper pots. All together this is the largest treasure ever to be found in the British Isles.

9.6

The object I find significant is the sewing machine. It is significant for the effects it had on women in the home, and on the clothes and fashion industry.

Let me give you some background information. The Singer Sewing Machine Company started in 1851 but it wasn't until 1857 that the first real domestic machine, in other words, machine to be used in the home, was made. In 1870 the company sold over 170,000 machines and this increased to something over half a million machines by 1880. By about 1913 or so, over three million machines had been sold around the world.

These machines revolutionized, that is, completely changed, domestic life for many women. Before it took about 10 hours to make a simple dress, but with a machine it took about one hour. As a result, women had more free time, and some women did sewing for other people to make a bit of extra money.

On the other hand, these machines meant that mass production of clothes was possible and many women went out to work in factories where they suffered poor conditions such as long hours and bad lighting, as well as low wages and a loss of independence.

9.7

1 The Lewis Chessmen are particularly famous for the grumpy-looking queens.
2 Mirrors were highly-prized objects.
3 Before the invention of the match, lighting a fire was time-consuming.

9.8

1 Mirrors were made of highly-polished stone or metal.
2 The tunic of the Hoxne pepper pot was loose-fitting.
3 Some of the chessmen are fierce-looking soldiers.
4 Only a highly-developed society could produce such beautiful objects.
5 Before the invention of the sewing machine all clothes were handmade.

9.9

1 The chess set represents the coming together of three important cultures.
2 A game of chess is essentially a war game, a battlefield.
3 Perhaps the Lewis chess queens had toothache.
4 The object I find significant is the sewing machine.
5 These machines meant that mass production of clothes was possible.

9.10

My choice of a significant object is the humble match, in other words, the simple stick with a black or pink tip that is used to light fires. It is significant, I believe, because of the change it made to people's lives. Fire is something human beings cannot live without. We need it to cook food and to provide heat. Before the invention of the match in the 19th century, lighting a fire was a time-consuming and difficult process. But with the invention of the match, fires could be lit instantaneously, that is to say, people could cook their food or get warm immediately. Now that matches have been superseded, that is, replaced, by gas and electronic lighters it is easy to forget the significance of the simple matchstick.

10.1

1 Treat yourself to a relaxing cruise in the Mediterranean and enjoy a wonderful holiday on our luxury ship! Daytime visits to interesting ports, where our fully-trained guides will show you the sights. Delicious food served all day long! Fabulous evenings on the ship with entertainment. Shops with everything you need on board this fantastic cruise ship. CruiseWell Holidays will take care of you!
2 Fiji Community Holidays! Take part in this exciting project and make a difference to the local community. Help dig and plant gardens, or build huts. Learn traditional skills and some words in the local language at the same time. In this village we recycle as much as possible, use solar panels to heat the water, and all meals are made from locally-grown organic food.

10.2

OK, I think I'm going to start now. Good morning everyone. Today I'd like to talk about ecotourism. There are four parts to my lecture. First of all, I'll give a definition of the term ecotourism and I'll explain the principles of this type of tourism. Secondly, I'll give you an example of real ecotourism. In the third part I'll give you some figures about the financial impact of green tourism compared to tourism in general and, finally, I will conclude my lecture.

10.3

So, in this first section I'll discuss what ecotourism is. Well, it's responsible travel to natural areas. And what is responsible travel? This is travel which conserves the environment and improves the welfare or well-being of local people. There are three main principles to this idea. Firstly, ecotourism should minimize, that is make as small as possible, the effect on the locality. Secondly, ecotourism should improve or conserve the local environment. And thirdly, the local population should also benefit as a result of the tourism. Let's look at those principles in detail.

Firstly, minimizing the effect on the locality. This is done by making sure that the tourism is small-scale and that something is given back to the community through the projects carried out. No big hotels are built and local people are as involved as possible in the tourism.

Secondly, ecotourism conserves or improves the environment. It does this through education, conservation, and recycling. This is education of the local people and also the tourists who visit. Conservation of the environment means respecting it by, for example, using renewable sources of energy, like solar power, or avoiding unnecessary use of plastics. And recycling as much as possible is important too.

Let's think, then, about how the local population benefit. Well, this can be in financial ways, of course, by earning money from the tourists, but also through education, better schools, access to places of interest, better health services, and improved roads and other means of transport.

Now I'd like to turn to an example of ecotourism holidays. These holidays are organized all over the world, mainly to natural areas. Most importantly, each holiday must make a difference to the local community.

Let me give you one example: a ten-day holiday in Vietnam where tourists can learn about the local customs and culture and, at the same time, help the economy of the country. Only local guides are employed to show the tourists the sights and explain the different customs and culture. The tourists stay in locally-owned hotels and can buy souvenirs made and sold by the local community. In addition, the tour operator supports a charity which enables the poorest children to go to school and the company also helps protect some endangered animals. So, you can see that this holiday can make a difference to local people.

This leads me to the financial impact. In fact, there are some surprising and encouraging figures. An increasing number of people want their holiday to have a positive impact on local people and, as I've just said, ecotourism does this. Look at Figure 1. This shows the percentage of money from holidays that goes to the local community. As you can see, this figure is 95%. In comparison, for traditional package holidays, only 20% of the money spent reaches local people and for cruises it is even less than that.

So, finally, to summarize the main points of my talk. Ecotourism conserves the environment and improves the lives of local communities. I gave an example of a holiday in Vietnam which benefits the people living in that area in different ways. Finally, I presented some financial information about ecotourism.

So, to conclude, real ecotourism is a responsible way to travel, benefiting both the guest and the host. By that I mean both the tourist and the local people.

Someone said, 'Take only photographs. Leave only footprints.' I think this is a good principle, but I would like to improve it. I would say, 'Take only photographs. Leave some benefit for the local community!'

10.4

Many students have problems listening to lectures and longer talks in a foreign language because they find concentrating for a long time difficult. It's very easy to switch off and then not follow, or understand, what the lecture is about. If this happens, don't worry. Just start listening again. You can still pick up the other main ideas. I think there are three ways to do this. Firstly, listen for the signposting language which tells you that a new part or section is starting. Secondly, listen for keywords on the subject that you recognize. Then continue to listen to the talk from that point. Thirdly, at the end of a talk the speaker often summarizes what has been said. By listening for this summary you can find out what has been talked about, and what you might have missed. You can then find this information by checking the lecture notes of a colleague or researching it on the Internet.

10.5

1 In this section I'll discuss the importance of tourism for the economy.
2 Going back to my first point about the employment of local people.
3 This leads me to the third part of my talk.
4 I'd like to turn to the subject of money brought into the country.
5 Let's think about the disadvantages of tourism.

10.6

1 People who suffer from diabetes need to follow a careful diet.
2 The student was accused of cheating in the exam.
3 How many candidates applied for the job of research assistant?
4 Aziz did not agree with the other students on the best place for a holiday.

10.7

Switzerland is a popular tourist destination for many people. Situated in Western Europe, it is bordered by Germany, France, Austria, Italy and Liechtenstein. This landlocked country is perhaps one of the most beautiful in Europe. Tourists come mainly for the spectacular mountain scenery and enjoy easy access to some of the highest mountains in Europe, thanks to the extensive public transport system. In the winter the main attraction is skiing. Switzerland offers many top-class skiing resorts with a wide choice of ski runs for all levels of skiers, from beginners to advanced. The mountain regions rely on skiing as their main source of income. However, there is now a developing problem as a result of climate change. Average temperatures are rising, resulting in warmer winters and less snow. Without enough snow, winter tourism in the mountains will not be possible and the economic survival of these regions is at risk. The tourism representatives are reacting to these changes by taking several measures, such as installing artificial snow-making machines and developing resorts higher in the mountains where the temperatures are lower.

10.8

A So today we are looking at Rio de Janeiro as a tourist destination. I've asked some of you to prepare some background information for us. Perhaps we could start by asking the speakers to introduce themselves and their talks. Camille, would you like to start?
B Yes. In the first part, I'm going to talk about the history of tourism in Brazil and particularly how tourism has developed in Rio.
A Thank you. Eun Suk?
C In the second part, I shall be describing the financial impact that tourism has had in Rio. I'll explain how much money has been earned in real terms over the last 10 years.
D And in the third and final part I'm going to give a brief description of the main tourist sights in Rio and talk to you about new projects that have been introduced, for example, visiting the *favelas*, that is the very poor slum areas of the city.
A Thank you. So, perhaps we can get started. Camille?

10.9

Good morning and welcome. Today I want to talk to you about three main tourist destinations in Jordan. Tourism is a very important part of the economy in Jordan, that's why Jordan is investing a lot in this sector. Firstly, I will talk about the historical ancient sites, perhaps the most famous attraction of Jordan. Secondly, I will go on to talk about the natural reserves. And finally, I will finish with city tourism.

First of all, the historical ancient sites. Of course, Jordan is famous because of Petra, which is one of the new seven wonders of the world and a UNESCO world heritage site. This spectacular city in the rock receives millions of visitors every year. But there are many other ancient sites, for example, Jerash, Madaba and the desert castles.

Phonetic symbols

Consonants				
1	/p/	as in	**pen**	/pen/
2	/b/	as in	**big**	/bɪg/
3	/t/	as in	**tea**	/ti:/
4	/d/	as in	**do**	/du:/
5	/k/	as in	**cat**	/kæt/
6	/g/	as in	**go**	/gəʊ/
7	/f/	as in	**four**	/fɔ:/
8	/v/	as in	**very**	/'veri/
9	/s/	as in	**son**	/sʌn/
10	/z/	as in	**zoo**	/zu:/
11	/l/	as in	**live**	/lɪv/
12	/m/	as in	**my**	/maɪ/
13	/n/	as in	**near**	/nɪə/
14	/h/	as in	**happy**	/'hæpi/
15	/r/	as in	**red**	/red/
16	/j/	as in	**yes**	/jes/
17	/w/	as in	**want**	/wɒnt/
18	/θ/	as in	**thanks**	/θæŋks/
19	/ð/	as in	**the**	/ðə/
20	/ʃ/	as in	**she**	/ʃi:/
21	/ʒ/	as in	**television**	/'telɪvɪʒn/
22	/tʃ/	as in	**child**	/tʃaɪld/
23	/ʤ/	as in	**German**	/'ʤɜ:mən/
24	/ŋ/	as in	**English**	/'ɪŋglɪʃ/

Vowels				
25	/i:/	as in	**see**	/si:/
26	/ɪ/	as in	**his**	/hɪz/
27	/i/	as in	**twenty**	/'twenti/
28	/e/	as in	**ten**	/ten/
29	/æ/	as in	**stamp**	/stæmp/
30	/ɑ:/	as in	**father**	/'fɑ:ðə/
31	/ɒ/	as in	**hot**	/hɒt/
32	/ɔ:/	as in	**morning**	/'mɔ:nɪŋ/
33	/ʊ/	as in	**football**	/'fʊtbɔ:l/
34	/u:/	as in	**you**	/ju:/
35	/ʌ/	as in	**sun**	/sʌn/
36	/ɜ:/	as in	**learn**	/lɜ:n/
37	/ə/	as in	**letter**	/'letə/

Diphthongs (two vowels together)				
38	/eɪ/	as in	**name**	/neɪm/
39	/əʊ/	as in	**no**	/nəʊ/
40	/aɪ/	as in	**my**	/maɪ/
41	/aʊ/	as in	**how**	/haʊ/
42	/ɔɪ/	as in	**boy**	/bɔɪ/
43	/ɪə/	as in	**hear**	/hɪə/
44	/eə/	as in	**where**	/weə/
45	/ʊə/	as in	**tour**	/tʊə/

ACKNOWLEDGEMENTS

Illustrations by: Kathy Baxendale pp.23 (human skin); Mark Duffin pp.34, 46;
Chris Pavely pp.10, 12, 15, 27

*The publisher would like to thank the following for permission to reproduce the following
photographs*: **Alamy** pp.4 (students on the grass/Rob Judges Oxford); 4 (University
in Istanbul/Holger Mette); 5 (radio presenter/Roger Bamber); 9 (Technical
University of Hamburg/Andia); 15 (banana tree & fruit/Eye Ubiquitous; 24 (10
pin mini usb mains charger/studiomode); 24 (e-reader/Vicki Beaver); 24 (mobile
phone/PSL Images); 35 (healthy foods/Corbis Premium RF); 37 (electron
micrograph/PHOTOTAKE Inc); 40 (Elizabeth Garrett Anderson/Mary Evans
Picture Library); 42 (Carl von Linde/INTERFOTO); 52 (ancient wheel/View
Stock); 52 (Lewis chess set/DWD-photo); 54 (Singer Automatic sewing machine,
1890s/North Wind Picture Archives); 57 (lit match/Radius Images/Corbis);
58 (cruise ship/Ruth Peterkin/Alamy); 59 (gap students/David Cole); 60 (Benidorm/
Jon Arnold Images Ltd); 61 (student and class/Image Source): **Ancient Touch**
p.52 (old Roman mirror/Ancient Touch); **British Broadcasting Corporation**
p21 (BBC Sports News); **British Museum** p.53 (Hoxne pepper pot/The
Trustees of the British Museum); **British Telecom plc** p48 (BT Infinity/
photo of house/Henrik Knudren); **Corbis** pp.45 (Jonas Salk in Lab/Bettmann);
55 (coffin from tomb of Tutankhamun/Robert Harding World Imagery):
Getty pp.21 (Manchester United/Patrick Stollarz/staff), snooker Mark
Williams/Michael Regan/staff); 40 (19th century medical items/Mary Evans
Picture Library/Alamy), 42 (Architects/Doug Menuez): **mashallah.design** p24
(e-ball connector); Oxford University Press pp.9 (dictionary/Oxford University
Press); 16 (female journalist/Oxford University Press/Digital Vision);
17 (broadcaster/Blend Images); 24 (MP3 player/Oxford University Press/
glowimages); 39 (cereal in bowl/Oxford University Press/photodisc); 42 (firefighter/
Oxford University Press/digitalvision); 58 (New York/Oxford University Press/
photodisc); 63 (Petra/Oxford University Press/photodisc): Photolibrary Group
pp.4 (lecture theatre/Stefan Kiefer); 4 (two male students/Paul Cox/ArabianEye/
Corbis); 6 (students and teacher/moodboard/Alamy); 22 (burrs on denim/Richard
Choy/Peter Arnold Images); 29 (two businesswomen/Ocean/Corbis); 30 (students
outside/Eric Nathan/Britain on View); 31 (students in classroom/Radius Images);
47 (man using mobile phone/Image Source/Alamy); 63 (man skiing/Fancy): Science
Photo Library pp.22 (Cocklebur (Xanthium) seeds/Dr. Richard Kessel & DR.
Gene Shih, Visuals Unlimited); 22 (hooks and loops material/Eye of Science);
41 (model of DNA/Will & Deni McIntyre); 41 (Penicillin tablets/Cordelia Malloy;
The Oxford Times p19 (magazine cover).

The Publisher would like to thank the following for permission to reproduce photographs:
Courtesy Toohey, K.S., Sottos, N.R., Lewis, J.A., Moore, J.S. and White, S.R. Self-
healing materials with microvascular networks http://sottosgroup.beckman.
illinois.edu/papers/nrs061.pdf, Nature Materials, 6, 581-585 (2007). Image
created by Janet Sinn-Hanlon, Beckman ITG, UIUC p.23 (self-healing plastic).

*Although every effort has been made to trace and contact copyright holders before
publication, this has not been possible in some cases. We apologise for any apparent
infringement of copyright and, if notified, the publisher will be pleased to rectify any
errors or omissions at the earliest possible opportunity.*